D1174630

Themes for English B

J. D. SCRIMGEOUR

THEMES

FOR ENGLISH B

A PROFESSOR'S EDUCATION IN AND OUT OF CLASS

The University of Georgia Press   Athens and London

Published by the University of Georgia Press
Athens, Georgia 30602
© 2006 by John David Scrimgeour
All rights reserved
Designed by Mindy Basinger Hill
Set in 10.5/14.5 Minion
Printed and bound by Thomson-Shore
The paper in this book meets the guidelines for
permanence and durability of the Committee on
Production Guidelines for Book Longevity of the
Council on Library Resources.

Printed in the United States of America
10   09   08   07   06   C   5   4   3   2   1

Library of Congress Cataloging-in-Publication Data
Scrimgeour, J. D.
 Themes for English B : a professor's education
in and out of class / J. D. Scrimgeour.
        p. cm.
A collection of the author's essays.
ISBN-13: 978-0-8203-2847-8 (alk. paper)
ISBN-10: 0-8203-2847-2 (alk. paper)
I. Title.
PS3619.C756T47 2006
814'.6—dc22   2006005466

British Library Cataloging-in-Publication Data available
*Many names have been changed to protect the privacy
of those concerned.*

For my students

CONTENTS

ACKNOWLEDGMENTS

These essays were written with the support of the Salem Athenaeum and Salem State College. I am particularly thankful to Salem State College's faculty writing workshops, in which many of these essays were composed.

Versions of several of these essays have appeared in other publications: "A Good School," *Boston Globe Magazine*; "Breathing" (under the title "People on the River"), *Chronicle of Higher Education*; and "What One Knows: An Appreciation" (under the title "An Appreciation"), *Thought and Action*. "Spin Moves" originally appeared as a chapbook published by Pecan Grove Press. An excerpt from "The Swans of Charter Street," "The Clock Is Half a Pair of Glasses," appeared in *Organica*, and "Living the Outfield" won the writing about baseball contest sponsored by *Creative Nonfiction* magazine. I also thank the Horace Mann Lab School for permission to publish the poem "A Spoon," by four of its students, and Caitlin Corbett for permission to publish her six cinquains in "Tilted."

Several people have supported and assisted the writing of this book: John Adams, Jay Atkinson, Patricia Brady, Brian Brodeur, Patricia Buchanan, Kevin Carey, Steven Carter, Scott Chiasson, Caitlin Corbett, Kristen Corcoran, Bill Cunningham, Donald Cutler, Jon Davies, Bryan Desjardins, Francis Devlin, Richard Elia, Alan Feldman, Charlotte Gordon, Elizabeth Hart, Gregg Higgins, Jennifer Jean, Patricia Johnston, Rod Kessler, Mary T. Lane, Doug Lang, Diane Lapkin, Thomas Luddy, Kathleen McDonald, Wendy Mahoney, Megan Marshall, Kim Mimnaugh, Deborah Oliver, Pamela Perkins, Arthur Riss, Jamie Scrimgeour, Xanthi Scrimgeour, Anita Shea, Dan Sklar, Jane Tompkins, Paul Tuttle, and Patricia Zaido.

Thanks to the Association of Writers and Writing Programs for giving this book its award for creative nonfiction, and to Robin Hemley, the judge who selected it. Thanks also to the people at the University of Georgia Press for guiding the book into print.

A special thanks to Paul John Eakin, whose encouragement and example have been invaluable, and to my parents, James and Christine Scrimgeour, two of my most important teachers. My two sons, Aidan and Guthrie, have already taught me more than almost anyone, and this book was written with an eye toward their lives and futures. And, finally, thanks to my best reader, Eileen FitzGerald, a better teacher than she knows.

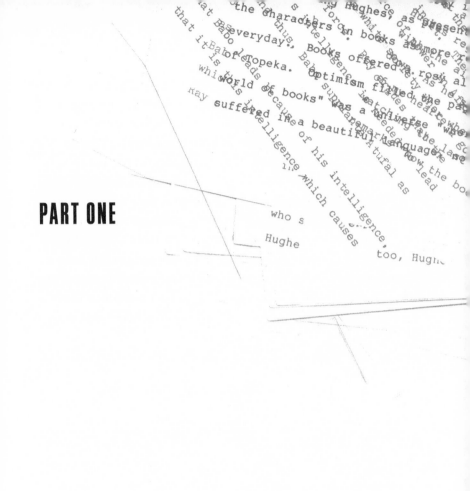

PART ONE

BREATHING

Only in winter, through a tangle of leafless branches, can I see from my office window the two smokestacks of the coal-burning power plant that rise over the city of Salem. Light beige, with soot smearing the upper parts, they seem the tallest structures north of Boston. A white light blinks atop the highest chimney every second or so like a heartbeat. The city's air quality is bad, and the plant is one of the major reasons. It is one of Massachusetts' "filthy five," plants that, because of their age, were exempted from legislation regulating pollution levels.

When I accepted a job to teach at Salem State College, my family and I moved to this city, and both my son Aidan and I developed asthma. That first winter and spring, Aidan, just one year old, had to have a machine—a nebulizer for infants—pump an airy spray of Albuterol four times daily into his lungs, including once in the middle of the night, to ensure that his airways stayed open. At first Aidan resisted, and we, not wanting to aggravate him and exacerbate his breathing problems, simply held the mask near his face, hoping he'd breathe in some of the vapors as they dispersed into our apartment. Eventually, we had to pin him down over his screams. Thankfully, he grew to like the treatment and even found it soothing.

Once, before my asthma had been diagnosed, I let my class out early and had my wife pick me up at the campus to rush me to the doctor. I could hardly breathe. In class, I had been coughing my way through a poem, wheezing at every line break. Granted, it could have been anything that made me suddenly asthmatic at age thirty, but whenever I look at the stained smokestacks, or notice the layer of black grime on cars or windows, I blame the power plant.

My first semester at the college, one of my students told me about an uncle who was a serial killer and buried his victims' bones in his yard. That surprised me, even shocked me—then. I suspected that she was putting me on. Now, having taught here for six years, such information would barely register. "Really?" I might say. "Huh." This past year, I had five students with bipolar disorder and one who was married to a gay man for fifteen years. One of my best writing students attempted suicide.

There was one part of the serial-killer story that was unusual: as my student told me, "they wrote a book about him." A book! The story was more sensational than the unrecorded miseries of many of my students—struggles with abusive boyfriends, poverty, addictions of friends and family members, and, of course, car accidents (it must be a Salem State graduation requirement: car demolition—three credits). It is as if the foul air from the looming power plant, slowly choking our children, has seeped into the students, making their lives—but not their souls—hard and bitter and unhealthy.

If only their suffering weren't so anonymous, and their accomplishments were recognized. Every year, Salem State graduates dozens of students who are parents. A few years ago, an unmarried Harvard student with a child got involved in a custody battle, and the *Boston Globe* ran a series of stories on her. No paper spotlights the unwed parents at Salem State, and they rarely have anyone fighting to take care of their kids. When their children wake up sick and can't go to school, they bring them to my classes, where they can hear a discussion of Langston Hughes's "Little Lyric (of Great Importance)": "I wish the rent / was heaven sent."

How much I owe these students, how much I have learned. They know the score; they know they are losing by a lot before the game even begins, and they shrug, as if to say, "What am I supposed to do, cry?"

Salem State students don't perform as well on standardized tests as Harvard students do. So what? They can tell you where to go—or not to go—to get your car fixed. I ask a student whose stepfather is a mechanic, "Be honest: do they rip you off?"

"Yeah," he replies, "sort of. They just tell you that you should replace lots of things that don't really need replacing. They make you buy things you don't need."

Make you buy things you don't need. Like a diploma from a private university. Make you want to be something you're not. He knew the score.

I leave my car unlocked. It's a piece of junk, a thirteen-year-old station wagon that qualifies as a compact car in today's age of SUVs. It's even got an old tape player, and I leave a bunch of tapes—most without cases—in plain view. No one's ever bothered with it.

In class, I pass out a page from a William Carlos Williams lecture on poetry. "I was going to copy the whole essay," I say, "but we can't afford it—budget cuts." I shrug. "Call your congressman."

At a recent meeting with a committee of outside evaluators of the college, a Salem State faculty member described our students as heroic. I knew what she meant. The faces under the cheap, rented mortarboard at graduation are those of heroes. A degree from Salem State means something: it often means one has endured. If, in most circles, it means less than a degree from Harvard, it also should mean more.

But wait. Heroic? Late last semester I walked into my seminar class—the only seminar I've ever taught at the school—and no students were there. Eventually four of the eight found their way, but only one had done any of the reading. Thinking fast, I got a James Baldwin video from the library, and we watched it, watched him saying, "The starting point, the bottom line is, *We are all brothers.* If you can't take it from there, you can't take it at all," his eyelids flashing, eyes pushing out from their sockets.

Every few months, I come across an article by or about an inspiring teacher (usually of high school English) that reminds me that what I do is valuable and honorable. And yet, the day-to-day realities often overwhelm: the students who disappear, the ones who probably will, all the missed classes. I work with troubled students, and what makes their lives seem even more tragic is that they're smart—smart enough to know they're troubled. You would not believe me if I listed what my students have endured in the last year alone: a mother's botched brain surgery; the death of a sister—a mother of two—and the subsequent alcohol binge of the father; car accidents (several); a sister's overdose; a mother jailed for dealing; bouts with anorexia, depression, drugs. . . . Then there are the "nontraditional" students—adults who have already made it through cancer, divorces, foster-home childhoods, homelessness, madness. Misery upon misery, often endured while working two jobs.

Unavoidably, their struggles seep into my own life. One semester I got several harassing phone calls from—I found out long afterward—a student's jealous ex-boyfriend. I never quite got used to the haunting Police song "Don't Stand So Close to Me" droning through my phone or, when I refused to pick up, playing on my answering machine at 12:30 in the morning.

Out my office window, the drab window shades of Meier Hall stare back at me, some off-white, some curdled cream. Beyond them, Salem State's own smokestack, which three years ago malfunctioned and spewed ash all over the neighborhood, rises out of the administration building. And just past that, the Sullivan Building, over a hundred years old, squats as if it knows something heavy, something true. Or perhaps it's just hunkering down, pressure squeezing the bricks off the facade.

I'm in it for the long haul. Last spring, the letters arrived, first from the college president, then from the board of trustees: tenure. With any luck, I'll get raises and promotions down the line, and my family and I will be able to afford life.

Aidan and I, five years older, are both much better. I take a puff from my inhaler before basketball at the Salem Y; he hardly ever needs one. We've acclimated. Our lungs have come to accept what floats between us, around us. We'll both probably die early because of it, the grit of this world.

I wonder if, in the years to come, I will still get teary at Salem State's graduations. The ceremony is simple, the setting plain. In the hockey arena, traces of sweat from the last season mingle with spring's scents drifting through the open doors. The deans, having practiced, pronounce the names—Tuttle, Corcoran, Brodeur, Carney—almost correctly, though they fail to drop the r's. The ice is long gone, the silly banners draped about, and many of our graduates are absent, too busy to show up, going about their lives amid the sting of the unclean yet human air of this historic city.

A GOOD SCHOOL

It's late afternoon, and the car battery dies while my family and I are at Salem Willows, the amusement park–turned–arcade down the road from Salem's power plant. I need to teach an evening class at Salem State College, and a long walk stretches ahead of me. An older couple that had driven over the bridge from Beverly for a bag of popcorn (a Willows' specialty) sees my distress and offers to drive me home. It's out of their way, but they do it cheerfully. On the ride, they find out I'm a professor at the college.

"Our niece went there. She loved it," the man tells me. I'm not surprised. Most people I meet in and around Salem speak appreciatively, even enthusiastically, about the college—either they went there, or they attended one of the theater productions, or they took a night class. This couple's niece had initially attended some well-known school and had disliked it. At Salem State she had small classes taught primarily by professors, not graduate students or part-timers. Her professors knew her name. "It's a good school," her aunt says.

A good school. It's a phrase I first heard in high school, when I was deciding where to apply to college. Thanks to good SAT scores, I received invitations from many colleges, most of which I had never heard: Case Western Reserve, Haverford, Bucknell. These, I was told—by my mother and by the savvy students in my Advanced Placement classes—were "good schools." If I wondered how someone who had never visited these schools could declare with utter certainty that they were "good," my doubts were erased by examining a guide to colleges, which labeled these schools "highly" or "extremely" competitive.

But what was a "good school"? I'm not sure the answer was clear to me as a prospective student or to the people writing the guides, for that matter. Only one impression was definite: a good school was one that people wanted to be in and where they felt a sense of importance. These schools weren't all the same; some promised personalities. If you attended Oberlin, you could feel that you were more of a free spirit than if you attended Amherst. Most important, though, if you went to a good school, you could take pride in it because it was a place that many people wanted to go to and not so many were accepted. To get accepted meant that you were among the chosen.

The Ivies seemed the most prestigious, and I ended up at Columbia University, drawn by the teeming streets of New York, and fascinated by James Simon Kunen's account of the 1968 student takeover in his *Strawberry Statement*. Of course, it also was important that Columbia had chosen me.

The distance between Columbia and Salem State at first seems too great to merit a comparison. Columbia is a world-renowned university, with a price to match. Salem State is an affordable public college in a state whose government cares little about public education. The students at Columbia are generally high achievers, graduates of top private and public high schools from accomplished and educated families. Many students at Salem State are first-generation college students from the less-affluent towns north of Boston. Many aspire to be nurses or high school teachers.

At Columbia, as at other good schools, it is presumed that one will get a "good education," another mushy phrase. According to the college guidebooks, a good education can be quantified: number of publications by faculty, number of books in the library. In its annual ranking of colleges, *U.S. News and World Report* weighs most heavily a school's endowment and the percentage of applicants it rejects. Just a smidgen of thought reveals how superficial and insignificant these numbers are. In my undergraduate education at Columbia, only a handful of professors inspired me. The most influential one I had only by accident, when he replaced a more famous professor who took a midsemester leave of absence after suffering a nervous breakdown. Did I count professors' publications before I enrolled in their classes? Did these publications make a whit of difference to my classroom experience? As an English major, I was one of fifty to a hundred students in the class. No one knew, or seemed to know, whether I showed up.

At some prestigious schools, underclassmen rarely get into classes with the prestigious faculty, and are taught instead by graduate students or adjuncts, part-timers who often shuttle among three or more campuses, collecting a pittance for their labor. Last summer, I had brunch with some faculty at Red's Diner, another Salem institution. Our waitress mentioned that she was thinking of going back to school and was considering Salem State. We got to talking. She had gone to Boston University for a year and hated it. Now in her midtwenties, she had recently returned from traveling and working in South America, and she had been taking courses at a community college. "And you know what?" she said, "I took two classes with the same teachers I had at B.U. And I was paying how much at B.U.?"

Mainly, a "good education" seems to mean that a diploma from the school makes you eligible for a "good job." *A good job.* A former student shares a bit of wisdom: in Los Angeles, everyone asks where you're from; in New York, everyone asks what you do; and around Boston, even if you're middle-aged, everyone asks what college you attended. When I think about how these attitudes affect my students, part of me is infuriated at the injustice. Yet another part of me thinks it is just as well. Why have our students strive to join that "good" world? If people are superficial enough to believe that money buys a better education, we want nothing to do with them anyway, do we? For the people I meet, like the older couple who gave me a lift, Salem State is a "good school." Is that enough?

What is the difference between Salem State and Columbia? At Salem State, accessible professors teach many of the students' courses, the classes are generally smaller than those at Columbia, and students aren't conferred a sense of entitlement upon graduation. Of course, there are also the other students: at a school like Columbia, which is devoted to accepting high achievers, one's classmates can be inspiring. It's not so easy to develop lifelong bonds at Salem State, where fellow students often rush to their cars after class to get to work or pick up their kids. I wish I could grant them the leisure to live the contemplative life that Columbia offers. Yet being among Salem State students, who often scramble to pay for school and try, not always successfully, to squeeze in the time to go to classes, can be eye-opening and inspiring as well. During the latest war in Iraq, I asked a class—"How many of you have a friend or relative over there?" Only two students out of twenty did not raise their hands. I wonder what the numbers would be in a Columbia classroom.

I meet Tony on the back elevator in the library. He's in his midthirties, wearing the blue striped shirt of the maintenance workers, "Anthony" scripted in a white oval on the breast. We exchange hi's.

"You teach here, right?" he asks.

"Yeah, English."

"I took all my English classes," he says. "I'm a history major. I want to teach high school, go back and work with all those teachers I gave a hard time." He smiles.

"Good luck," I say.

When I get off the elevator, I'm still thinking about Tony. It isn't that he is so unusual—a full-time maintenance worker who is also a full-time student; it is that he is, it seems, so wonderfully typical here. The same person who is keeping the buildings up is taking classes in them. The gap between the blue-collar employees and students is so much smaller at Salem State than at all those schools I desired to attend. In this case, the employee and student were one and the same. And, better yet, he wanted to return to his community, to become a teacher.

What is there to say? I work at a good school.

THE SWANS OF CHARTER STREET

THE PARLOR

. . . this primitive town.

MARY PEABODY, writing about Salem

On top of a bookshelf in the small library of my sons' elementary school in Salem is a bust of Horace Mann, the nineteenth-century educator and reformer often referred to as the father of public education in the United States. The school, like many American public schools, is named after Mann, but he had been dead thirty-seven years when it was founded as a training school for the Salem Normal School. The school changed its name in 1937 as a way to celebrate the centennial of Mann's appointment as the commonwealth's first secretary of education in Massachusetts, an appointment that marked the beginning of the public education system in the United States.

In 1837, after being appointed secretary, Mann thrust himself into his work with messianic zeal. In his position, he wrote controversial annual reports that shaped the way the commonwealth and nation came to view public education. These widely read reports were persuasive in part because of Mann's fervor and skilled rhetoric. He writes of one crumbling schoolhouse, "already aware of the danger, the mice have forsaken it." The reports were also persuasive because of the dedication of their author. Mann visited school after school in an effort to determine the state of education and the best course for it to take. He was thorough.

He was vilified by those who did not like his progressive approach—he wanted to fund education with taxpayer money, and he wanted all students, regardless of class, to experience the best education, together, in public schools. This education, Mann felt, must be based on sustaining a child's natural delight in learning and the pleasures of knowledge. It discouraged corporal punishment and encouraged exploration, the development of the whole person. He mentions a Philadelphia businessman who saw students only as future employees and wished that they know simply "how to count to 100 and row a boat to New Orleans." "If others had not known vastly more than this," Mann writes, "there would have been no dollars to count, nor New Orleans to go to." (Mann's words have an eerie echo after the devastation of Hurricane Katrina.)

The bust was a gift to the elementary school from the Normal School class of 1937. From a distance, it is elegant and does justice to the handsome Mann. Looking at it, one wouldn't know of Mann's prematurely white hair, which turned when he was 36 after the early death of his first wife. Shoulders back, neck straight, he stares directly into the sunlit room, lips tipped into a faint smile, confidence and wisdom emanating from him.

The bust is yellowed, like coffee-stained teeth. If you tap it, you find that it is not marble but metal. The tinny echo reveals it to be hollow. Across the base, the name "HORACE MANN" was carved inexactly by a long-ago college student, as if with a putty knife. It provides an odd contrast to the finely sculpted face, marking the artistry with a touch of the human.

A few weeks ago my younger son, Guthrie, a kindergartener, reported that kids were claiming there was a ghost in the boys' bathroom.

"A ghost?" I asked. "Are you scared?"

"No. I don't think it's true."

The ghost, the school librarian tells me some days later, was Horace Mann. Some children had come to this conclusion, and it had led to a run on the books the library had about Mann. She laughs. "One student came up and asked me, 'Did he die here?'"

Mann died a long way from here, in Yellow Springs, Ohio, but he did know Salem. He walked its streets, praised its schools, and courted his second wife, Mary Peabody, at her family home at 53 Charter Street, a house that still stands in the heart of this scarred city. He wasn't the only famous person to marry into the Peabody family. Mary's younger sister, Sophia, was courted by Nathaniel Hawthorne in the same house. And it was in this house that the eldest sister, the important intellectual, reformer, and educator, Elizabeth Peabody, first met Hawthorne and helped launch his ascent to literary fame.

The house's illustrious past is obscured by the present. On the outside, at least, it is in disrepair. Painted a drab gray streaked with greenish-black mold, it seems smaller than my family's modest box on Winthrop Street, and, somehow, uglier. It looks as if a semi rumbling down Charter Street could make it collapse, but it has been standing for well over 150 years. If it was larger, more majestic, one could say that it loomed over the ancient Charter Street burying ground beside it, but its three stories seem small, dwarfed by the new glitzy arches of the Peabody Essex Museum across the street. Just a year ago, the museum brought piece by piece from China Yin Yu Tang, an eighteenth-century merchant's house, and reconstructed it. The Peabody house faces the back of the Yin Yu Tang, two hundred years of east and west separated by a one-lane street. Though the Chinese house is its nearest neighbor, the Peabody house seems more fastened to the adjacent graveyard, squatting like a large gray monument anchoring the western corner of the grounds. The Salem Witch Memorial, a small rectangular walkway with hewn rock benches carved with the names of each of those put to death in 1692, anchors the eastern side. The graveyard holds the dust of notable early figures, such as John Winthrop, the first governor of the colonies, and Hawthorne's great-great grandfather, Colonel John Hathorne, Esquire, one of the judges of the witch trials.

When my family moved to Salem, we rented a house on a street named after the judge—Hathorne Street—a block from where I live now. Salem was more affordable than many of the surrounding communities. Unlike its whiter, more affluent neighbors, it was gritty. When I arrived to interview for the position at Salem State, the shuttle driver who took me to my hotel from the airport told me how the city "had been really depressed. It's coming back a little now."

We took to it right away, even if its polluted air helped trigger asthma in our year-old son and me. We walked the Common, we used our Salem residency to get into the Peabody Essex for free, we took Aidan to story hour at the library. When he was healthy enough, we'd take him to nearby High Street Park, the tiny grassless park littered with glass and dog droppings behind St. Mary's Italian Catholic Church, and help him down the slides.

That first fall I would often walk the mile from our house to campus. When I would cross the bridge over the commuter rail tracks, I would occasionally see in the swampy pond off to the left two swans, their whiteness as bright as fire against the murky reflective water. The encroaching houses, and even the roar of a train to and from Boston every half hour, did not scare them away. They seemed a good omen, a small mark of beauty on this place that seemed like it could become my home.

This place, Salem, is old. The city is 150 years older than the United States. Most houses that have historical plaques on them are over 150 years old ("Built for Joseph Cox, Merchant, c. 1810"). On that walk to the college, I pass a house on Jefferson Avenue with an unofficial plaque, hand-painted letters reading "Built by Horace + Henry Michaud 1946." Salem residents would get the joke.

In the unkempt graveyard at the end of my block are the bodies of people who lived three hundred years ago. Many of their names are unreadable now, worn off the old stones. Many of the stones themselves have sunk into the ground, almost buried by three centuries of dirt. Some have fractured and broken; unconnected letters and letter fragments lie about. The town is so heavy with history that no one seems concerned about the loss of a few names every decade or so. No one famous is buried here. I take my sons to the graveyard in the winter to sled down its faint hills. There needs to be enough snow so that you don't feel the bump of the small stone protrusions, little aches of past, on the way down. For an adult, there needs to be a lot of snow.

If you squeeze through where one of the bars is missing from the graveyard's black iron fence, you will be in the parking lot of the local senior center. The building used to be an elementary school, and before that it was the original site of Salem State, when it was founded in 1854 as one of Horace Mann's normal schools for teachers. Angle through the lot, cross the street, and head down Cambridge Street, where the modestly well-off live in their tiny antique houses. One block and you reach a vestige of aristocratic Salem, Chestnut Street, broad and tree lined, with grand brick mansions of architectural splendor; it has been called the most beautiful street in America. Its houses, built some two hundred years ago with Salem's great wealth from its shipping industry, routinely sell for well over half a million dollars. It is still the street for Salem's elite, though now they aren't ship captains but lawyers (Horace Mann's first profession), financial advisors, and literary agents.

The distance between Chestnut Street and my family's modest house is far more than the two physical blocks. It is the distance that moved Mann to revolutionize public education, to challenge the ignorance that class prejudice fosters. And the cruelties of this distance, the abuse of power and privilege in his own ancestors, is why the city haunted its native son, Hawthorne.

Born here on July 4, 1804, Nathaniel Hawthorne grew up secluded and doted on by his family, and dreamed of becoming a poet. He lived the majority of his life in the city, though he seemed to dislike it. The aristocratic Salem clashed with Hawthorne's democratic tastes; he "preferred gin to champagne," recalled an acquaintance. Yet, as he explains in "The Custom House," Hawthorne's autobiographical introduction to *The Scarlet Letter*, he is drawn to Salem. His attachment comes from two centuries of ancestors who lived and died here, whose flesh has turned to the dust that spots his shoes as he walks the city's streets. Hawthorne says this attraction is the "mere sensuous sympathy of dust for dust." He will be dead someday, and Salem seems to invite that death. He acknowledges that there is a sentiment within him—"not love, but instinct"—to live in the Salem of his forefathers, yet it is this sentiment that convinced him to leave. "My children have had other birthplaces," he writes—and one hears his sigh of relief—"and, so far as their fortunes may be within my control, shall strike their roots into unaccustomed earth."

Like Hawthorne, I had ancestors here in 1692. Their history has been recorded by my father, himself a poet and teacher. As he followed the tourists' red line painted on the sidewalk past shops full of occult and pagan trinkets and curios, my father, moved by our ancestors' spirits, composed a long poem that blended then and now. One of my ancestors, Mary Towne Estey, was killed for being a witch. Another, Thomas Perkins, served on the jury that sentenced her. The persecuted, the judging. The victim, and the one too ignorant or timid to resist lies. There are no accusers in my line, no unrepentant judges. Hawthorne's guilt is not mine. My second son was born in Salem Hospital; his roots have been struck in Salem's dust.

Yet the city haunts me, too. It is hard to reconcile Salem's past with its modest, worn present. There is no narrative that binds the hangings of 1692 to today. The city does not cohere. Hawthorne's essay, "Main Street," which Elizabeth Peabody published in a journal she founded, shows how ungraspable the city was, even in his time. In it, a showman presents a rather two-dimensional pageant of Salem's past while being heckled by an audience member who finds the show obviously phony and simplistic. In the end, the props tumble, and the pageant never gets completed.

The red line on the pavement can't go everywhere, can't tie it all together in an epic loop. It leads tourists from one historic site to the next. It passes the Peabody house but does not point to it. It does not go close to Gallows Hill. The aristocrats, save those on Chestnut Street, have fled. Salem State College, the center of my city, serves the harried working class. The red line is a good long mile away from its industrial brick.

For me, the voices from Salem's past are too numerous, too loud. It is an *old* city, and the voices merge, cacophonous, with the voices of Salem today—my children and their classmates on the slab of asphalt behind their school, my own struggling students, their writing full of rough music. My father was drawn to our blood ancestors, but I'm drawn to those who do what I do: Horace Mann, the educator, and Hawthorne, the writer. So I step into the nineteenth century, into the house on 53 Charter Street, and sit with Elizabeth, Mary, and Sophia Peabody, with Mann, and with Hawthorne. The babble, for a time, diffuses. They are sturdier than I, and smarter. I'm glad that Sophia, despite her frailty, has come down from her room to join us. It must be the presence of the pensive Hawthorne (my wife can't get over how handsome he is). A talented artist, Sophia draws in the sketchbook on her lap while we converse. I wish she would ask to sketch me, though I'm a bit afraid of what her eye might reveal.

Mary, the middle sister, is the family beauty, but in a social circle that doesn't particularly value looks, she's less of a force than her older sister, Elizabeth, with her powerful intellect, or Sophia, with her seductive sensitivities. Mary has a cleverness with words, though she uses them less often than Elizabeth. Her comments bring appreciative smiles from Mann, which only she—and perhaps Hawthorne—sees. She's more practical and socially conscious than Sophia. When the two younger sisters went to Cuba for a year so that the invalid Sophia might convalesce, Mary was appalled at the slavery she witnessed. Sophia sketched and flirted with the men.

Headstrong Elizabeth has an almost superhuman energy. She is, by all accounts, an inspirational teacher, though it has been said that she lacks a system and is not enough of a drillmaster. Her hair does not stay tucked, but she does not notice, though the others do. She speaks and listens with a fervor that is energizing and a bit terrifying. She has been talking with some of the transcendentalists, especially Mr. Emerson, and, as usual, is bursting with ideas.

Have I been invited?

Even though the conversation is about education, it is lively. A year ago, Mann abandoned a promising law practice and political career to become the commonwealth's first secretary of education, the first such post in the nation. Almost every friend thought him foolish to take such a low-paying job ($1,500 a year, no expenses) with such little prestige. He has just found out that, after debate, the legislature in Boston voted to renew his fixed contract. "Well, one thing is certain: if I live, and have health, I will be revenged on them; I will do more than 1,500 dollars worth of good," he says, and smiles, his white hair aglow in the lamplight. He wants to restore the old custom of educating the rich and poor together, and, to that end, wants public schools as good as schools can be made. He despairs at the public's lack of interest in his idea. He will speak on it tonight at the Lyceum in Salem, and hopes that more than a handful will turn out.

Elizabeth, who has helped Bronson Alcott run the infamous Temple School in Boston and has published important works about progressive education, encourages him. She's working on her own ideas about education, ones she will eventually put into a scandalous essay, "The Dorian Measure." She will write that public education deserves great sums of money. "It is plain," she'll say, "that if we can spend a hundred million dollars a year for so questionable a purpose as the late war with Mexico, we have resources on which we might draw for public education." And schools should educate the whole self, the spirit of education should be "purely human"; though the common wisdom finds it absurd, she wants to teach gymnastics, dance, music, and art to public school students.

Hawthorne listens, unconvinced. Although he graduated from Bowdoin College, his education has always come from his own reading, all the books that his sister brings him from the Salem Athenaeum, a private lending library, about the history of his family and city. He recalls a line from his journals: "All really educated men, whether they have studied in the halls of a University or in a cottage or a workshop, are essentially self-educated." He does not say it in this company, but will share it with Sophia on one of their walks.

It is time for Mann's lecture. All rise to get their coats. Unbeknownst to me, Sophia had been sketching me. Now she shows me what she's done, then folds her sketchbook and whisks it upstairs. I'm so startled by how far my hairline has receded that I don't look carefully at my own face.

Horace Mann became the father of public education in the United States by visiting thousands of schools and writing reports that Mary, not yet his wife, generously volunteered to recopy and edit. Report after report after report. When Mary and Mann had their first child, Sophia said of her nephew, "I suppose his first words will be a school report." Having endured several meaningless "assessments" of Salem State, I find it hard to imagine more drab work.

But his work had meaning. It was worth it. By the time he left his position, in 1848, to fill the congressional seat left vacant by the death of John Quincy Adams, Mann had established the public education system in Massachusetts, and several other states were busy building a public school system modeled on his example. There would be no going back.

I read Hawthorne and feel the heaviness of the city's bricks, coated with history and ambiguity and soot. I read about Mann's work, and breathe the possibilities of Emerson, ache with the birthing of new generations. The writer and the reformer, wrestling the past, sculpting the future. Both wise, both obsessed in their ways, both married into perhaps the most impressive Salem family ever, a family of modest means, but remarkably talented women.

Just down the block from the Peabody house, Hawthorne's statue stands on a grassy island between streets, absorbing the weather. He, like Mann, looks confident, sure of himself, despite the oblivious traffic angling past him.

Mann sits in a brightly lit room, his name attached to schools throughout the country, though, like the street names in Salem that mark the city's ancestors, few know who he was, or what he did. Handsome, but yellowing, he staunchly surveys what he has wrought.

SCHOOL REPORTS

All great acquisition comes from voluntary thought.

ELIZABETH PEABODY

When I visit a ninth-grade class at Lynn Technical High School, we need to meet in the school library, since a student just vomited in the classroom. I have them sit in a circle and I read some poems. They don't seem especially interested, though the librarian behind her counter seems appreciative. It doesn't feel like it's going well, so I reach into my bag of tricks and prepare to recite a slangy poem about basketball, one I know from memory. "This is the poem of mine that's probably closest to rap," I say, desperate.

"Rap? What's that?" a Latino ninth grader says to me, straight faced. He's been one of the interested ones, a talker.

I pull up for a second. Did I see him smile? I smile. I catch my breath. What do I know of today's music? Does rap still exist?

"You know," I say—his words are an education—"I'm not really sure what rap is anymore. You probably know more than me. You could tell me."

He's silent, but not defiantly so. I go on.

Later, I attempt a writing exercise with them. I talk about the distinction between concrete and abstract language, and how lots of poets try, in Emily Dickinson's words, "to give abstractions shape" by imagining an abstraction as something tangible—Hope is a bird, for instance. I read them my poem about Sorrow playing right field for the Red Sox, we make a list of abstractions on the untrustworthy chalkboard that's been wheeled in for me, and then I ask them to try a poem of their own, working with one of the abstractions that we named.

The exercise was a bit rushed, but I was still disappointed in the students' inability to understand it. Only two or three of the class of twenty got the concept. Many of them came up to me and asked me to read their poems with the question, "Is this right?" I'd read a poem heavy with abstractions and oozing sentiment.

"Well, it's not really what I asked you to do, but it's fine," I'd say. "I'm glad you're writing."

They would look at me, completely confused. Was it right? Did they do it correctly? And if not, their faces seemed to ask, how could I say it was "fine"? I'm not sure what was more troubling, their inability to understand the assignment, or their concern with doing a poem "right."

"All ideas outside the book were contraband articles," wrote Horace Mann on his own education. It was something he hoped to change.

"Buckle Down" reads the cover of the MCAS workbook on the desk of the tenth-grade teacher at Lynn English High School. The MCAS (Massachusetts Comprehensive Assessment System) tests are the controversial high-stakes standardized tests that have become the measuring stick for public schools and the gatekeeper for high school graduation in Massachusetts. Students take the major versions of the test in fourth, eighth, and tenth grades. They must pass the tenth-grade test to receive a high school diploma.

Around me dark-skinned kids and a few light-skinned European immigrants wait, a bit nervously, for the class to begin. I am a guest lecturer, there to read some poems and talk about poetry.

Like death, poetry is a great equalizer. I meet with what has been designated a low-level class—these kids weren't going to college—and with a few honors classes. In general, the "average" kids pick up more. When I read Yusef Komunyakaa's poem, "Venus's Flytraps," they understand the lines, "One afternoon I saw what a train did to a cow" and "My momma says I'm a mistake." They note the surprise of "I wonder what death tastes like."

I have a photo from that class that the teacher took with a digital camera and printed in black and white. I'm in the center of a group of tenth graders, standing behind a table, grinning a bit stupidly, perhaps a little too openly happy. I don't have my usual bad posture, my shoulders hunching toward my chest. Instead, I seem propped up by the students around me. The fingers of my right hand appear on the shoulder of a smiling, heavyset white kid in a denim jacket. My left elbow hangs on the shoulder of a Latino with a baseball cap on backward and crossed arms. He's smiling, too. The kids are mostly my size, though some are already taller. There are far more boys than girls, almost all black or Latino. Probability tells me that one or two might make it to college, if that. Who?

Let my children go. As soon as my elder son entered kindergarten, I heard the drumbeat of standardized testing, distant but audible. At the school's first parent-teacher organization meeting I attended, they discussed fundraising and how to improve MCAS scores.

When I look at the MCAS tests, I'm heartbroken. Here's the prompt for an essay question on a recent fourth-grade language arts exam:

> You woke up one morning and learned that it was snowing. School was closed for the day! It was a dream come true. Suddenly you had time to take a break from the usual routine and do what you wanted to do.
>
> Write a story about a snow day off from school that you remember. Give enough details in your story to show what you did and how wonderful the day was.

Where to begin? First, let's wince at the vague "learned that it was snowing." Isn't "saw" more accurate, cleaner? Then, let's groan at the weight of the clichés in the rest of the paragraph: "dream come true," "time to take a break," "usual routine." And isn't "usual routine" redundant?

The second paragraph: "Write a story about a snow day off from school that you remember." Will fourth graders (or even adults), seeing the word "story," assume they are supposed to write fiction or nonfiction? I suspect more will lean toward fiction—they may have heard that an essay is nonfiction, a story is fiction—and the first paragraph implies that the experience is to be imagined. So, they prepare to write fiction, but now it must be about what they "remember," to tell about what they "did." Hmm. Are they supposed to tell the truth or not? It sounds like they should write about what really happened, but isn't that an essay? A fourth grader could be stymied by such poor wording. And, as critics of this question have pointed out, what if students have never experienced a snow day? Who writes this stuff?

Apart from the writing, there's another problem, the problem of assumptions. Who says a snow day is a "dream come true" for kids? For kids whose parent or parents work, the day could well be difficult and tedious. The secretary in my department used to bring her kids in to the office, where they would read or play video games for eight hours. Yippee!

Even more troubling than the question's assumptions about stay-at-home mothers with hot chocolate and SUVs are its assumptions about school itself. Implicit in the question is that school is not a fun place to be, so missing it is "a dream come true." Yes, with or without tests, a school day can be drab, but why enforce that idea on an exam every public school child in the state must take? Both my sons like Horace Mann Elementary. Of course, they haven't taken the MCAS tests yet.

I wish that essay question was an aberration, but on that same exam is the poem "Homework," by the fine children's writer, Jane Yolen. "Homework" has a child speaker who intends to do various disagreeable things—cleaning the litter box, taking out the garbage—to avoid her homework. Each stanza in the poem suggests that school, and the homework it requires, is unpleasant, something that we do out of obligation, out of compliance. It is followed by series of enervating questions that seem designed to prove this point:

You can tell that this selection is a poem because it is

A. short and funny.

B. written about children.

C. written in verse and contains rhyme.

D. written in simple language.

To the final question, "*What is the theme of 'Homework'?,*" a kid might reasonably answer: Learning sucks.

The MCAS tests—indeed most tests—do more harm than good. They make appalling presumptions about human nature, and their high profile tends to force these presumptions on people—to make them believable. Standardized tests, at least in their current incarnation, in which they are used to reward and punish schools, teachers, and students, imply that humans respond to the most basic and dull Skinnerian prompts: see candy, push lever; push lever, avoid electric shock. Am I doing this right? Have I made it to New Orleans? Push lever, push lever.

When did I realize this? It was not from my own testing experience. I never would have gotten into an Ivy League college without my SATS. And, surprisingly, it wasn't from having children and envisioning their educations—school can be deadening with or without tests if one worksheet follows the next. No, it has been from teaching at Salem State, teaching working-class students who—in class—are clearly bright, and who—out of class—are clearly wiser than students I taught at the supposedly "elite" private university, DePauw, Dan Quayle's alma mater.

My students' work at Salem State is often sloppy; sometimes it doesn't get turned in. Several students each semester, including some of the best, don't make it through to the end. But these problems, I have come to realize, are because the students are constantly forced to make choices, to weigh each part of their lives and decide which to put down and which to shoulder.

I was speaking recently to an adjunct faculty member at the college who would be teaching for the first time. She ran by me her idea for her opening composition assignment: she was going to give her class a few articles about George W. Bush's proposed exploration of Mars and ask them to write a paper about whether it was a good idea or not. I thought about it. It wasn't a topic I would have chosen, but why? I imagined student responses. At a school like DePauw, most of the students would have launched right into the assignment. *Here's what the country should do! I have the answer.*

At Salem State, the student response would be much different. Most would feel awkward about writing such a paper, partly because they have not always been encouraged to believe that their opinion counts, and partly because they would humbly realize—in a way that DePauw students wouldn't—that they don't know nearly enough to be able to say anything intelligent about the question. This recognition lies in a wisdom that students at more prestigious colleges lack. What the hell do any of us know about the exploration of Mars? Although they might not be able to articulate it, my students would comprehend the artificiality of the assignment, and, implicitly, they would question its significance. Should they ask for time off work and lose out on some seemingly necessary cash to do a good job on the paper, a paper about outer space? What to shoulder?

The classroom in Horace Mann Elementary School in Salem is dark when I step into it. A flash—a mouse (Horace Mann's mouse?)—scurries across the floor and disappears. I'm here to talk to my son's third-grade class about poetry. Soon, the light flicks on, and the children march in, bands of paper around their heads. They are magnets, with an N and an S on either side of the bands. They are, at their teacher's command, repelling or attracting each other. When they repel, they stand with arms folded, staring sternly at another student a few feet away, or, they have their back turned to another. When they attract, they put hands on each other's shoulders.

I'm introduced, and, after I ask their names, I begin talking to them about imagination. What do they think of when I say that word? Purple dogs. A rubber chicken dancing on a plate. I talk about Wallace Stevens, how he felt the imagination works with reality, how the ordinary, the everyday, like a snowman or a blackbird, can be amazing and surprising. "There are many truths," I say, quoting Stevens. The students list some ordinary things—an eraser, a chalkboard, the ceiling—and I read them a poem about muffins that my college students composed: "Ten Ways of Looking at a Muffin." Then I take some scissors and hold them up—"How about these? What do these make you think of?"

And they're off: it's a person who is always talking. It's tired of eating paper all day. It's an alligator. I can hardly rein them in.

A few minutes later, we break them into small groups, and they're off again. In the group I work with, Aaron asks if he can do a poem of his own about an eraser. He already has "got some" for it. I want to say yes, but we're on task. "Later. Let's do a clock now. Everyone try and come up with some things." Aaron walks across the room and curls up behind an easel, composing his own ways to look at a clock. His writing, it turns out, is so rudimentary that he can't read what he wrote. The words are far from how they are spelled: K-l-o-k. But he lists ten ways, numbered and all. ("Amazing," his teacher tells me later.) The clock looks like a marble, he says, the clock is like a head, a balloon floating in the sky, the clock is the world.

When we gather together, we listen to the poems each group has composed. Here's one by Aidan, Daniel, Shanteliz, and Yanisha:

A Spoon

A spoon could be a metal teardrop for the Tin Man.

A spoon is like an asteroid on a stick.

A spoon is a weird mirror that makes you look upside down.

It can be a teeter-totter for food.

Or a catapult for banana wars.

A metal diving board.

A tool to eat poisonous food that may not touch your hands.

A drill to make a hole in a wall of mashed potatoes.

A shovel to dig up a dog's bone.

A gavel in a courtroom.

A reflex hammer to break a tiny house in fruitland.

A sled for George.

A balance beam for a baby chick.

It could be an upside down snake.

Something to grow flowers on.

A mirror to check your teeth.

An umbrella at the beach for an ant.

A periscope to spy on people.

A spoon is the pencil with which I wrote this poem.

We all applaud after each poem, and the groups take questions and comments. Then, I answer some questions about poetry, about being a writer and a teacher. We have to stop before I can answer them all. It's time for lunch.

I am failing these children. I'm encouraging them to think that there are not right answers, only interesting ones—a clock isn't one thing; it can be many. Although I dropped the word *metaphor* into the discussion a few times, I'm not teaching them the word *verse* or *stanza*, or that poetry rhymes, all of which are expectations for the MCAS. In fact, they're discovering that poems don't necessarily rhyme, that poems can be lies, that poems can be fun, that school and learning can be joyful. Or, to put it another way, using something ordinary from their lives: school is like a magnet; it can repel, or it can attract.

THE SHORE

I love the notion of living near the dead.

SOPHIA PEABODY

I have lived in Salem for almost eight years, longer than I have in any other place. My sons have ground the city's dirt into their knees and elbows diving for baseballs. They have swallowed some of its dust. My wife can find most yard sales without a map. The absence of street signs amuses rather than annoys. The city has become home.

The college, too, has become home. When I hear that in a recent study Massachusetts ranks forty-ninth in the nation in spending for public higher education, I grimace, but I don't send out my résumé. My students are trapped in a state that, ironically—given Horace Mann's legacy—scorns public education on every level. The children of Chestnut Street are whisked off to private schools before kindergarten. When they are teens, they meet with tutors, angling for higher SAT scores. The kids at my son's school ride a bus to an old, poorly lit Salem State gym because their school doesn't have its own gymnasium. Their aged building is, according to the superintendent, barely adequate. And by the time some of these public school students enroll at Salem State College, they have endured years of the world telling them—based on standardized test scores and empty pockets—that they are barely adequate. The students from private schools fear and pity them. It amounts to a psychological war.

How the past echoes! In her loving biography of her husband, *Life of Horace Mann*, Mary writes about an early convention on education that Mann held in Salem, one that did not go well: "One gentleman, who made one of the first speeches, questioned the expediency of endeavoring to get the educated classes to patronize public schools. He spoke, he said, in the interests of mothers who preferred private schools for their children; and he believed the reasons that they had would always prevail: they would have their children grow up in intimacies with those of their own class. No one spoke on the American side of this question."

It is February 2004. I am walking the icy streets of Salem. I want to feel the spirit of Horace Mann, the one I sensed in the school that bears his name, the one where third graders wrote me a class thank-you poem about a heart: "A heart," my son contributed, "is a bouncy ball. I played with it yesterday." But whether it is the chill of the winter, or the ghost of the MCAS tests, or the fact that Mann, despite his bust, was just a visitor here, it is Hawthorne's spirit that haunts, with his doubts about improving human nature, his sense that this city, old even in Hawthorne's day, drains creativity. It is Hawthorne, not Mann, who is Salem's ghost, he who wrote about it. Though he finally fled the city, his is the name of the city's main hotel. There are Hawthorne Animal Hospital; Hawthorne Cove Marina; Hawthorne Tours; Hawthorne Ear, Nose & Throat Specialists; and Hawthorne Oil.

I'm coming from the college, heading downtown to lunch with a colleague, our new Hawthorne scholar. I walk along the shoreline, trying not to look at the power plant chuffing its soot across the harbor, until I come to a secluded cove. There, just over a stone wall, I see them: five—no six—swans resting on the gravelly sand. Two are yearlings, brown feathers mixing with white. They all startle, and I stop walking. There are no boats out on the rough, cold waves, but mallards are everywhere in the surf before me. They gambol like children in the polluted water. The swans flutter back to a rest, orange beaks bright against their papery necks. Their webbed feet are half-buried in the sand and broken glass and damp paper scraps; their bodies hover above it all, like glorious ideas.

If there are such things as ghosts, let these be them, spirits of the company I kept in the Peabodys' parlor back in 1838. The tourists will never see their grace, the political hacks on the Board of Education will never know how rich they make this gritty world.

But let these be simply swans, too, soon to fly north to a secluded lake somewhere far from here. Let their children be born elsewhere. *There are many truths.*

I keep walking, and the swans let me pass. Eventually, I veer away from the harbor, end up in front of 53 Charter Street, the Peabody house. Although it qualifies for one, it has no commemorative plaque. The owner, a descendant of the Peabodys, has allowed the outside to deteriorate, apparently to spite the city. Rumor says it is beautiful inside. The day has wavered between clouds and sun, but now it has gone as gray as the house. A few raindrops. Those nights when he first felt the stirrings of love, Hawthorne might have stood where I stand, having taken leave of Sophia and her sisters, perhaps after walking them home from Mann's lecture. In the darkness he senses but cannot see the grave of his great-great-grandfather, the name carved firmly and exactly, as befitting such a prestigious man. He sighs, and his mind turns to the evening he has just spent—all this talk of education, Sophia's friendly eye. The lights are on in the Peabody house. Shadows cross the curtains. For a moment, he could be any man in love, hopeful for his future, however vague its outlines.

Horace Mann did not drink, smoke, or use foul language, yet he was on to something. Friends thought him foolish for forsaking money. At the age of fifty-three, when he was a U.S. congressman, he had the opportunity to become governor and perhaps president. Instead, he passed on these conventional ambitions and took the position of college president out in the boonies of Ohio at a school that was just opening, a school that in 1853 was one of the first coed schools in the country, Antioch College. Yes, like Hawthorne, he left Massachusetts, but he also stayed put—committing himself to learning and teaching, often against long odds. He and Mary Mann wrote the wisest words I have ever read about education: "In a republic like ours, children must be educated . . . so as to be above pride as well as above abasement."

Neither man is wrong. Hawthorne said good-bye to the city and spent much of the rest of his life in Europe. He concludes "The Custom House" by writing of his "decapitation" as a Customs House officer, his removal from office when a new administration was voted into Washington. "The moment when a man's head drops off is seldom or never, I am inclined to think, precisely the most agreeable of his life," he writes, but for him, it was a blessing. It freed him from Salem, and it freed him to write again. He had to leave his civil life to renew his writing life.

What to shoulder? Am I losing myself in the whirlpool of the classroom? In the heaviness of Salem, its thick past and ignorant present? Didn't I, like the young Hawthorne, dream of being a poet? Across the street, the wall of Yin Yu Tang is as white as an absolute answer. I pull my gloveless hands from my pockets and grasp the black iron fence surrounding the Charter Street Cemetery. Depending on the angle from which you view me, I look like either a prisoner dreaming escape or an outsider hoping for entry. What I see, though, are only my own hands, curled and cold, scarred from basketball at the Salem Y—all those hands groping for a ball for . . . for what? These hands that hold chalk, that mark student papers and poems, chapped and wrinkled at the knuckles. I hardly recognize them.

At my feet, the red line needs repainting. Perhaps, though, it would be better if it just disappeared, gradually flaking off onto our soles, then falling off them, too, somewhere. The specks would land where they land, traveling with each new step, each rain, mapping a new path impossible to see or follow. It is an imaginary path of course, but it spans the distance from the brick sidewalks of Chestnut Street to the marijuana butts in High Street Park, from China to Charter Street to Salem State. The path even stretches through the doors of my son's elementary school, past the kindergarteners' self-portraits, to the bust of Mann, that old gift sitting among books and children and mice, eyes perpetually open.

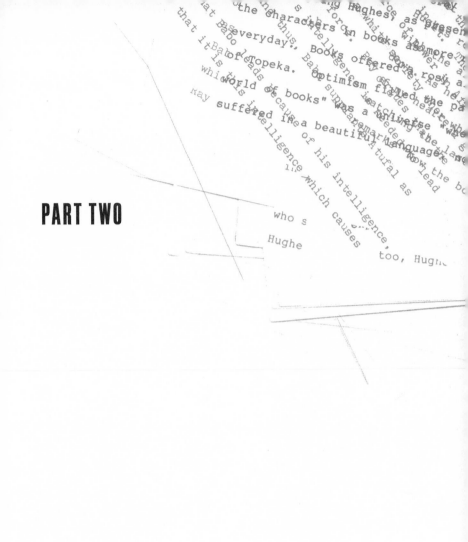

PART TWO

ME AND LANGSTON

AS I LEARN FROM YOU, I GUESS YOU WILL LEARN FROM ME

I, too, sing America.

LANGSTON HUGHES

The first book I ever bought that wasn't for a class was Langston Hughes's *Selected Poems*. It was the fall of 1984, and I was in my junior year at Columbia University. A week earlier, a friend had lent me a copy of Hughes's book, and I had immediately felt an affinity with the author. Just coming to the art of writing poetry myself, I found Hughes's simplicity appealing, and his knowing, jazzy rhythms—developed in the first half of the twentieth century—still seemed to echo those of the city that pounded and skittered outside my dorm room. His work was a kind of dictionary to help me understand all I had been experiencing since I had come to New York. Suddenly, the rhythms from the boom boxes teens carried down the street, and the black English that at first had felt like a foreign language, seemed not just appealing but valuable, aesthetic. Of course, Hughes's poems didn't have the current vernacular. I didn't hear people saying "Good morning, Daddy! / Ain't you heard / The boogie-woogie rumble / of a dream deferred?" but I heard their echoes on the basketball courts down in Riverside Park, where I'd go when Columbia wore on me: "Yo, that brother ain't got no game."

I read and reread his book, turning to the sepia cover every now and then to study the photo of Hughes. He smiled up at me, his body turned away from a desk and typewriter, middle-aged belly rounding out his shirt. His slicked-back hair looked strange. None

of the blacks I saw on the streets every day had hair like that. Was it
a conk, a hairstyle achieved through a painful process to make one
look more white? It was a style that, Malcolm X had pointed out,
seemed a sign of self-hatred. It sure looked like a conk, but Hughes's
poems had made me like him so much that I couldn't believe it. As
it turns out, I was right. Hughes was light skinned, and photos in
his biography show that his hair had always been more wavy than
frizzy. Hughes had, like me, attended Columbia, though he left after
one fairly miserable year.

Hughes's autobiography, *The Big Sea*, begins with him at twenty-
one, on the crew of a ship leaving New York, setting sail for Africa.
As the ship pulls away from the city, Hughes stands on the deck
and tosses all his books into the sea—"all the books I had had at
Columbia, and all the books I had lately bought to read," he says in
the opening paragraph. He had been more excited about New York
than Columbia to begin with, and the university did not make him
feel welcome. He was only assigned housing as a freshman in 1921
because the school did not know he was black. When he arrived,
officials consulted, phone calls were made, and he was finally given
a room. When he tried out for *The Spectator*, Columbia's newspaper,
the editors cruelly assigned him to gather frat house and society
news: he would never have been allowed into any frat. Hughes spent
that year reading books, going to shows, and attending lectures at the
Rand School of Social Science. He immersed himself in New York,
especially Harlem. Why go to school, when he could be getting an
education? He claims that he missed an important exam to attend
the funeral of Bert Williams, a great black vaudeville star. He had
his priorities right: art (or is it death?) before grades.

Hughes traveled to Africa going the only way he could: as a mess
boy on a steamer. It is hard to imagine an act so devoid of the usual
ambitions. Who in the Ivy League now would forego an education
for such unclear and unpromising prospects? Yes, a few bohemian

souls might try it, but they would do so with the safety net of family money to fall back on. In an unfinished story I wrote during my year in graduate school at Columbia, the male narrator decides to leave his studies at Columbia and light out across the country. I got him as far as Grand Central Station, drinking a gin and tonic and talking to a woman as he waits for the train. I couldn't go on. I couldn't dream of such a move, even in fiction. Still, I, too, left Columbia. Of course, my escape took five years, and they had to reject me for the doctoral program to make me go.

Hughes wrote briefly about Columbia in *The Big Sea*, and in one of his more famous poems:

Theme for English B

The instructor said

> *Go home and write*
> *a page tonight.*
> *And let that page come out of you—*
> *Then, it will be true.*

I wonder if it's that simple?
I am twenty-two, colored, born in Winston-Salem.
I went to school there, then Durham, then here
to this college on the hill above Harlem.
I am the only colored student in my class.
The steps from the hill lead down into Harlem,
through a park, then I cross St. Nicholas,
Eighth Avenue, Seventh, and I come to the Y,
the Harlem Branch Y, where I take the elevator
up to my room, sit down, and write this page:

It's not easy to know what is true for you or me
at twenty-two, my age. But I guess I'm what

I feel and see and hear, Harlem, I hear you:
hear you, hear me—we two—you, me, talk on this page.
(I hear New York, too) Me—who?

Well, I like to eat, sleep, drink, and be in love.
I like to work, read, learn, and understand life.
I like a pipe for a Christmas present,
or records—Bessie, bop, or Bach.
I guess being colored doesn't make me not like
the same things other folks like who are other races.
So will my page be colored that I write?
Being me, it will not be white.
But it will be
a part of you, instructor.
You are white—
yet a part of me, as I am a part of you.
That's American.
Sometimes perhaps you don't want to be a part of me.
Nor do I often want to be a part of you.
But we are, that's true!
As I learn from you,
I guess you will learn from me—
although you're older—and white—
and somewhat more free.

This is my page for English B.

   While this poem may seem autobiographical, Hughes deliberately
distances his own life from that of the narrator. The speaker, unlike
Hughes, does not get a dorm room but must stay at the Harlem
Branch Y. And Hughes was not from Durham, but from the Mid-
west. These changes make the speaker's life a bit more representative
of black life than Hughes's own. Blacks suffered discrimination in

housing, even if he, through some mix-up, did get a dorm room. And he was not one of the mass of southern blacks who migrated to northern cities. Although he lived for some time in Cleveland, much of his youth was spent in small towns. He was often one of a handful of blacks in primarily white schools. Yet though he did not grow up among the black masses, he would identify with them, changing facts from his own life to do so.

I'm a white associate professor teaching creative writing to working-class students at a state college in Massachusetts. And here I am, claiming an affinity to Hughes, wanting to see his life and mine converge. How many details I would have to change!

1986-87

I wish the rent
was heaven sent.
LANGSTON HUGHES, "Little Lyric of Great Importance"

I had just turned twenty-one when I graduated from Columbia University with a bachelor's degree in English. I had no idea what I wanted to do. I had become an English major for the simple reason that I could write moderately good papers faster than I could solve complex math problems. I did only about half the reading in my courses, and I came away with a B+ average. To me, this was simply proof that I was doing well. I was able to get by without nearly as much effort as the students around me. The baseball players I lived with were not a studying lot, but they still spent more time with their books than I did. Four or five of us would walk to campus, find an open classroom, empty our backpacks and hunker down with our chewing tobacco, spit cups, and homework. Then I'd drift. I'd read a few pages of a novel that I had to write a paper on—due the following week—then break out a notebook and try to write poems. Chew, spit, line break.

Although I had hardly spoken more than three words to any of my English professors—the classes were generally fifty to a hundred students—the Columbia English Department accepted me into its master's program, the only program to which I had applied. It was a one-year program, and my financial aid package explained that I was going to have to take out $11,000 in loans, and, in combination with my parents, pay another $5,000. In 1986 this was an astonishing amount (it's still an astonishing amount). The sum of my loans from my four years of undergraduate education, taking out the maximum amount each year, was about $10,000. In one year, I'd be borrowing more than I had in all the previous four.

Columbia was a gated community. The walkway that stretched through the center of campus, from Broadway to Amsterdam, had high black gates on either end, and the other entrances had gates, too, most of which were locked at night. The walkway spanned the base of a wide mountain of steps leading up to Lowe Library. When the steps weren't under repair, they held pockets of sitting students, catching sun during the day, drinking at night. Weekend mornings, there would often be broken bottles scattered at the foot of the statue of the Alma Mater, a black marble woman with a scepter in one hand and a book in the other who seemed to guard the entrance to the library. Lowe itself was actually an administration building more than it was a library. In the depths of that building, a windowless office among many windowless offices, I signed the papers. I agreed to take on those loans to attend graduate school at the university.

What a confused decision, one clouded by unconscious class values about public and private education. I can imagine my response if it had been a public university, one without the garlands of ivy draped over it. Sixteen thousand dollars to go to the University of Connecticut Graduate School for a year? Ha. Some years after Langston Hughes left Columbia, he ended up as a nontraditional student, attending the all-black Lincoln University in Pennsylvania after working in Europe and New York and Washington, usually as a waiter or busboy. The nontraditional students I have, oh, how they would smile hearing that I took out $11,000 for a year of school. Only kindness, or bafflement, would stop them from laughing aloud.

So what was I buying? It certainly wasn't a better education. A master's degree in one year? That sounds like a gimmick, something you'd get from an unaccredited school-by-mail in Arizona. In two of the four classes each semester, we were not required to do any work, or even to show up. All students who enrolled in the course received an "R" grade. I still don't know what "R" stands for. Registered?

I was buying that Columbia name. It was fucking expensive. I've always thought of that year as the worst of my life.

In the late 1980s, New York was not a good place to be. AIDS deaths were mounting, and rich and poor, black and white, were drifting farther and farther apart. In Brooklyn in December of 1986, Michael Griffiths, a young black man, was run over after being chased into traffic by a group of whites. Less than a year later, in Wappinger's Falls, a town of six thousand south of Poughkeepsie, fifteen-year-old Tawana Brawley was discovered in a garbage bag, feces smeared over her, "KKK" and "Nigger" scrawled on her body in black powder, some of her hair yanked off. She claimed that she had been held captive for four days, tortured, and raped. One of the white assailants, she said, wore a badge and a holster. Brawley's aunt, who felt that the case was being mishandled, called the New York media, and the case snowballed. Almost immediately, Brawley's veracity was questioned. Confrontations between Governor Mario Cuomo and Brawley's lawyers over the appointment of the special prosecutor led to Brawley refusing to testify under oath, and, without her testimony, the grand jury decided the charges were frivolous. For months, it was a major story in the city, and New York lawyers and demonstrators traveled by the busload to Wappinger's Falls.

The city seemed as ugly as the Brawley case, and as with the case, it wasn't clear who was responsible. Walking down Broadway, I had to zigzag through the beggars and through the shit of rich folk's dogs. In the campus housing where I lived, I'd often have to step over a sleeping man in our tiny vestibule.

Early in that school year, I sensed I was in the wrong place. Was it at the cocktail reception for new students, where everyone seemed comfortable? Where was someone I could talk to, and what did one talk about over cocktails? I would have sidled over to a discussion of the Mets' chances to make the playoffs—I was engrossed by their young, black talents, Darryl Strawberry and Dwight Gooden—but I didn't hear one. And it seemed somehow wrong to speak of sports. This was, after all, graduate school in English. As interested as I was in the Mets' fate, I was bored by sports talk and its obvious triviality. Where was Jack Salzman, the professor from my undergraduate years who seemed infused by literature, who exuded intensity when he asked his startling questions (On Ginsberg's *Howl*: "What are we doing reading this for a *class*?").

At the end of my first semester, I was to give a presentation on a critical essay about Melville's *Billy Budd*. Though thick with deconstruction, the essay seemed explicable to me the night before the class. I would just have to go slowly, use a few phrases from the essay to guide me.

In class, I chanced to sit at the foot of the seminar table, opposite the professor, an aging, white-haired man who seemed content to sit quietly through the class, like most of us. The seminar was full, and late arrivals took chairs along the walls. The professor offered a few opening words, then, looking down the table, gave me the floor. All faces turned to me (all white, of course—I don't recall a single black graduate student in English), and I began to plod my way through the essay. I had only gotten through the first two pages, one dense paragraph at a time, when what had seemed a bit fuzzy suddenly seemed incomprehensible. I talked in circles for a minute, then stopped.

"Just a minute," I said. I looked down at my notes. I looked at the photocopied essay, which might as well have been Latin. I looked at my notes. They did not cohere.

The silence grew. I kept my head down, my brown hair dangling across my eyes, and mouthed the words in front of me, hoping to reconnect them to sense, or at least to voice. But nothing. Silence. Heavy sweat. I shuffled my papers. A word, any word. A tear instead.

The professor spoke, "If you're not feeling well, we can go on."

I nodded, head down.

Sometime that same month, the December that Michael Griffiths died, I was writing an essay on Hughes's autobiography, *The Big Sea*. A classmate was writing on Zora Neale Hurston. She proposed that we go together one Saturday to the Schoenburg Library—the Harlem branch of the New York Public Library—to do research. She was a little shaky about going herself. We took the bus to Harlem and scurried through drizzle and black folks to the library doors.

Inside, we each went our own way. As usual, I didn't have a plan—instead, I drifted. I found and listened to recordings of Hughes reading his poems to jazz, and was disappointed. He sounded surprisingly flat, drab, and—how to say it?—white. What exactly had I hoped for? Something with the energy of the city's music, as I was hearing it: the coolness of Luther Vandross's voice, the bass licks of Marcus Miller, the funkiness of Rick James or MTUME. As an undergraduate, I'd seen some of these performers in concert. Often my friends and I were the only whites in the audience, clapping and hooting with the rest, though a bit reservedly. We didn't want to make a spectacle of ourselves.

The day slogged on. When we reunited at dusk to leave, my colleague, stammering, proposed that we take a cab. She clutched at her briefcase and looked imploringly (conspiratorially?) at me. Her fears had only increased from a day among courteous, quiet blacks, and, sensing her fears, I became a little jittery myself. We hurried from the library doors down the expanse of pavement to the street and flailed our arms over the gutters. A cab stopped and we propelled ourselves in.

A few weeks later, I received readers' comments on my Hughes essay. The professor under whom I had written the paper was kind enough, but the second reader, a young black professor, was brutal, saying that I lacked "critical sophistication" and "scholarly background." Hughes's book, he wrote, "gives us a series of fascinating stories that skillfully avoid the central issues of his work and his life. His autobiography is a thrilling tale of deception and seduction that reminds us of his extraordinary powers of narration and persuasion, and I get the sense in reading Mr. Scrimgeour's essay that Hughes has found another victim."

Things exploded on the Columbia campus in March, when something violent happened outside the Plex, the campus nightclub, as it was closing for the night. It is not clear what happened. I was not there. The next day, though, flyers were being put up all around the area—*MOB of 30 Whites attacks 6 Blacks*—read one. *WANTED*, read another, with a photo of two white Columbia students, *For inciting a race riot.*

Later that week, I stopped at an informational table set up on the central walkway through Columbia's campus at the foot of the stairs leading up to Lowe Library. There were flyers with bold "STOP RACISM!" headings, and taped to the front of the table was the poster of photos.

"What happened?" I asked.

A light-skinned black woman wearing glasses explained, "there was Darryl and Kurt and . . ." She rattled off six names, "and there were at least . . ." She turned and looked at a friend behind the table, as if wanting verification, "at least six white guys."

I didn't ask why the poster said thirty whites. This was a protest against Columbia, against white power; all around me, from the black and Latino cafeteria workers I'd worked with during my work-study job, to the struggling immigrants I'd tutor at Riverside Church, to the hustling white corporate traders, the world was showing that the cause was fundamentally right: black folks, and poor folks, were taking it hard; the rich were taking it easy. The poster may have been a lie, but it was a case of manipulating the truth to get at a larger truth. Still, something in me (the poet?) was appalled, and I vowed never to do that.

In order to save some money that year, I had made an arrangement with two undergraduates to share a room with them—a studio apartment. It was on the "garden level" of a fraternity house on 115th Street, just off Broadway. It wasn't a "real" fraternity—no secret handshakes or drunken revels—but it allowed us to get decent housing relatively cheap. I wouldn't need a room at the local Y. The size of a master bedroom, the room contained three beds, one desk, and a fridge that was almost always empty. My bed was closest to the outside wall. After I'd turn out the light and pull the shade, I'd listen to the occasional footsteps clacking on the sidewalk, less than ten feet from my head, just beyond the thick iron bars striping my window.

Late one night, I was awakened by a voice in the street. Someone was hollering at Kevin, who lived up on the fifth floor. I propped myself on my elbows and listened to the noise beyond the shade.

"Kevin," the voice bellowed, "Kevin, come down here!" I heard the vestibule door open, heard a person buzzing to be let in. I did not hear the click of the inside door unlocking, the person climbing the stairs. Instead, I heard the footsteps retreat to the street.

"Kevin . . . Kevin, you fucker, get out here." The voice sounded angry, but also hurt, betrayed, like a scorned lover.

"Kevin, you nigger lover, get down here."

I sat up and moved to the edge of the window. From my angle, I couldn't see the speaker, only his long shadow cast by the streetlight. I gently pushed the shade—less than an inch—trying unsuccessfully to glimpse who was yelling. I didn't risk moving the shade more, afraid that he would see motion and demand that I let him in.

I was also afraid for him. It seemed unwise to holler "Nigger" in the middle of a New York City street at two in the morning. Part of me was also troubled that hordes of blacks and whites did *not* descend on him and tear him apart.

Minutes passed, with him hollering occasionally, or returning to the vestibule and buzzing all the rooms. I remained propped uncomfortably on an elbow, wanting to lie back, but too tense, a cornered mouse. The door never did open.

What had happened? I found out later that there had been an argument between the drunk student outside my window and a black guy at Tom's Diner, two blocks down Broadway. Kevin, who knew both people involved, tried to calm things but, in doing so, took up for the black guy.

I didn't know Kevin well. I remembered him coming to the back of the bus after my last junior varsity baseball game and sitting next to me and talking as I brushed away tears. I knew that I wouldn't play the following year—I wasn't good enough—and that my baseball days were over. I knew it was a foolish thing to weep over, but the thought of my mediocre final season, and worse, that I would not catch the scent of the spring's first cut grass with such deep joy ever again, kept me gulping and pressing my head into my sleeve. Kevin reminded me of the good plays I had made that year (there weren't many). Looking back, it's amazing he remembered them at all—a diving catch, a double off the centerfield fence.

1984-85

Come,
Let us roam the night together
Singing.

LANGSTON HUGHES, "Harlem Night Song"

I had given up on baseball in the fall of my junior year, the year when I first read Langston Hughes's poetry. It was also the year I began to write my own. My story—which I have told so many times now that it is probably pure lie—is that I brought home a few "poems" to my family and handed them to my father. I didn't know what they were, only that I had spent an astonishing amount of time on an astonishingly few words. One I had written after waking in the middle of the night in the small, bare cinderblock dorm up on the northern edge of campus, the building closest to Harlem. In an insomniac blur, I scribbled several images relating to my grandmother, who had died the previous summer. The next morning, I typed it up, pushing some words around (this was still a few years from computers). A few weeks later, home for a weekend, I handed what I'd written to my father in our family's kitchen. "I wrote this," I said. "Is it a poem?" My father, a poet himself, read it, then he called my mother over and read it aloud to her, his voice breaking. When he'd finished, they were both weeping. "Yeah, it's a poem," he said.

Poetry. I knew this was something different, something alive, if only because I cared about it. A few weeks after my first rush of poems, I took the bus home to Connecticut one weekend and sat with my father in a diner across the street from the bus station, showing him my recent efforts. He read the pages eagerly, and I sipped my coffee, looked around at people in the other booths, trying to act casual. Every now and then I'd sneak a look at him. How disappointed and confused I was that he didn't immediately gush over this new work, these slivers of myself.

Hughes should have been so lucky. "A writer?" his father, James, had said when Langston told him about his ambitions, "A writer? Do they make any money?" James had left the family when Langston was an infant to make a fortune in Mexico, and Langston saw him only a few times during his childhood. James despised American racism, yet he also possessed a furious loathing for his own race. He warned against going to college in the United States, "where you have to live like a nigger with niggers." James's wealth enabled Langston to afford his year at Columbia, but his miserly behavior, and his disdain for his son's aspirations, made life difficult. Langston, he felt, should go to Europe to study engineering. James demanded itemized accounts of all his son's expenses while he was in school, and he threatened to stop paying tuition unless Langston's grades improved. When Langston decided to leave Columbia, he returned the last hundred dollars his father had sent him, and he never had contact with him again.

The fall I started writing was also the first semester I owned a stereo, a cheap Radio Shack tape and record player I'd gotten for about $150. Spending any more seemed like it would be indulgent, too much for pleasure. That same semester, a suitemate, whose wealth and social position was such that his sister's engagement was announced in the *New York Times*, brought to school a new bit of technology: a CD player. The music sounded clean, like the high-priced stereos I couldn't afford, but the most distinctive quality was that one could push a button and hear a song immediately. I almost winced the first time Yale (his real name) pushed a button midsong, expecting to hear a scratch. But no, it was able to leap from one song to any other, just like that. I was probably most astounded, though, to discover that this feature, the main distinguishing characteristic, made the price $1,000. That was half of what I had earned while working all summer mowing lawns, carting bricks, and pulling weeds. I would use my rewind and fast-forward buttons.

I would also, perhaps spurred by my own writing, declare myself an English major, and begin taking English courses. That spring, I took a lecture course on modern poetry with the well-known poet Kenneth Koch. From under his clump of vivid gray-white hair, he read the poetry of D. H. Lawrence or Ezra Pound or Rainer Maria Rilke aloud, and that was enough. Along with a term paper, we had to write imitations of some of the poets that we studied. I heard from a fellow student that Koch read my parody of Lawrence's "Snake" aloud to the class: "In Illinois August / with popsicles melting." I had skipped that class. Poetry had not made me a conscientious student.

Toward the end of the semester, I went to see Koch. I was trembling. He was the first professor I had gone to speak to in the three years I'd been at Columbia. I wanted to talk to him about my paper topic. I was interested in writing about Hughes, even though we had not covered him. "Isn't he rather simple?" Koch asked, trying to dissuade me. After getting an unenthusiastic OK, I asked if he would look at a few of my poems. He looked a little put out, but read two.

"So, I guess you want to get into the poetry workshop next semester?" he asked.

I was puzzled and a bit irked. I didn't even know he taught such a class. I hadn't planned to take it. And I didn't like his insinuation that I wanted something from him, at least something so crass as a favor. I couldn't have said then what I wanted, though I can see now that I simply wanted acknowledgment of my effort, a sentence or two of support: "Keep writing."

The semester of Koch's class, the spring of 1985, was marked by student protests at Columbia demanding that the university divest its holdings in companies that did business in apartheid South Africa. Hamilton Hall, a main classroom building named after Alexander Hamilton, the Federalist rumored to have "negro blood" in him, was barricaded, the main doors locked with chains. The protesters sat in front of those doors, making speeches and music, during the day, and sleeping, or not sleeping, through the frigid nights, huddled in their grimy sleeping bags. Classes, including Koch's, were generally still held, but students had to enter Hamilton through a narrow tunnel from another classroom building, bumping backpacks with students going the opposite direction.

I never stayed overnight myself, but I did lend my body to the cause, sitting on the wall that ran alongside the building (I was almost always alone; baseball players didn't do protests). I was there the day Jesse Jackson came to speak, and I was there several freezing nights, when, to keep motivated and warm, people would drum, and drum, building to a frenzy. Pounding mixed with high-pitched whistles, figures dancing in the brightness from the floor lights that had been set up in the crowd, their shadows shifting, huge against Hamilton Hall.

I never danced. I sat in the dark periphery, alternately watching and trying to record the images. I clutched a pen in my numb hand, the spiral binding of my notebook icy in my palm. Scribble, scribble, as the drumbeats crescendoed around me, like waves. Scribble, though I can't see what I'm writing, the dancers' shadows rising and falling, like waves.

Beyond me, in the darkness, the outlines of Columbia's campus loomed, darker still: the dorms, the main library that looked down on the grassy lawns. In 1921, when Hughes had attended Columbia, those lawns had been the university's baseball field. Lou Gehrig (who also left Columbia) had launched home runs there that reached Furnald Hall, the coveted housing across the campus where, in 1924, with the college president's tacit approval, students had burned a cross to drive a black student out.

The blockade ended after the university agreed to consider changing its investments. In a celebratory event, several hundred people left the steps of Hamilton Hall one evening in early spring and marched through the streets of Harlem, a block-long multicultural mass. As we passed record stores, they opened their windows and blared the tune, "Free-eeee Nelson Mandela." We ended up crowded into Harlem's Abyssinia Baptist Church. I was prepared for the second coming of Martin Luther King Jr. We got C. Vernon Mason, who would go on to become one of Tawana Brawley's lawyers, and a speech that was more heat than light—all placard, no poetry.

1982-83

Once, while he was impoverished in Venice, Hughes was visited by Alaine Locke, a famous black intellectual on the faculty at Harvard. Locke wanted to show Hughes the sights. Hughes was grateful, but, he says,

> Before the week was up, I got a little tired of palaces and churches and famous paintings and English tourists. And I began to wonder if there were no back alleys in Venice and no poor people and no slums and nothing that looked like the districts down by the markets on Woodard Avenue in Cleveland where the American Indians lived.
>
> So I went off by myself a couple times. And I found that there were plenty of poor people in Venice and plenty of back alleys off canals too dirty to be picturesque.

Back in 1982, as a freshman at Columbia, I endured new-student orientation, which included many icebreaker parties and events, the most formal of which was the freshman convocation. After climbing the steps of the building (Columbia has steps everywhere!), we went through the heavy double doors and into a large auditorium. Upperclassmen ushered us in, handing each of us a small baby-blue beanie with a white 86 on it. On our heads, they looked like bright yarmulkes, though I could not have used that word then to describe them—I hadn't learned it. Even wearing them backward, as I did, there was no way to look cool with a beanie. I sat squeezed between other freshmen I didn't know, too timid to strike up a conversation. The crowd silenced. A dean strode to the podium and welcomed us to Columbia. There was a joke or two, a lauding of the school and of us, but only two sentences from the speakers lingered. Nothing abstract about the glories of learning, or Columbia's tradition, just the warning from an academic dean as he described our environs: "To the east is Morningside Park. Don't ever go in there."

Although I couldn't have articulated it then, just like I couldn't have said the word *yarmulke*, these lines worked against all my hopes for Columbia. I had chosen a college in the hippest of cities to get beyond the social and psychological strictures of my small Connecticut hometown. And, upon arrival, I was being warned: "These are your boundaries." Hughes, of course, would have ignored these instructions, perhaps because he had no choice. I had a choice, and I chose what seemed then as prudence. With the exception of one or two uneventful daytime strolls along the park's fringes, I obeyed.

Sometime in that first week, I sat alone in my dorm room and turned on my roommate's stereo. Searching for something, I spun the dial through the FM stations and, suddenly, there it was, WBLS and its pulsing urban music. Disco had died; rap hadn't quite arrived. The music was infectious, danceable. Some warm afternoons I would just lie on my bed and listen, eyes unfocused on the ceiling, the *Iliad*, or Aristophanes, or my calculus textbook, closed on the bed beside me. The music wasn't about being loud, or being fast. It was about getting down, not moving up, and it helped me span the distance between black and white. The notes were my invisible steps down the hill, down into Morningside Park, down into Harlem, the Harlem Branch Y, where I take the elevator up to my room, sit down, and write this page.

During that orientation week the entire class took a placement essay exam in English. Despite my good SATs and the highest possible score

on the Advanced Placement English Exam, my essay landed me in
ENG 104, a low-level English class. Unlike most incoming students,
I would have to take a full year of freshman writing, rather than a
semester. My classmates were international students (I remember
one French guy who spoke almost no English) and a lot of minori-
ties. I still recall Jeff Simmons, a tall light-skinned black guy whom
I'd play basketball with occasionally at the college gym. Only recently
have I thought that the "B" in Hughes's poem might suggest that the
speaker, too, had been placed in a lower-level class.

In that composition course, as in most of my classes, I was a B+
student. What were my papers, my *themes*, like then? Certainly they
had very little of what I thought in them. I had been properly trained,
and I was eager to complete my work efficiently, without unnecessary
effort. I latched onto the first thesis that I thought I could support
and trotted out a series of examples as evidence. Point one, point
two, point three, conclusion, done. In the one essay I can actually
remember all these years later, I had argued for the insignificance
of social environment in identity formation. Parents, I wrote, are
the primary influence in children's development. I suspect that I
remember it because I felt uncomfortable turning it in. I had—what
was I thinking?—put a sliver of myself into it.

OLDER–AND WHITE–AND SOMEWHAT MORE FREE

For Langston

> *I, too, sing America.*
> LANGSTON HUGHES

America doesn't sing. Not much.
I love you this and that, and such,

it croons along to the radio,
but turn it off, there's no

melody, no voice, a silence
that t.v. and lunch

—the crunch of potato chips—
slip into. No dancing, no hips

shaking and thumping the air,
no splayed, unbuttoned hair.

Langston, you had the better ear.
I trust you when you say you hear

America singing, but come today
and listen, come now, today

and bury your pen in our throats—
those simple, sometimes angry notes

that made your line almost true:
America singing? That was you.

One time on the streets of New York, I was walking with my black girlfriend, a Haitian, daughter of an African diplomat, holding hands. A rather strung-out interracial couple came walking from the other direction, the black man's arm around the white woman's shoulder, and the man peered at us. "We should trade," he said, as our paths crossed. I think I gave a polite smile.

We were lovers for three years. She was premed, and I was prelost. I spent a lot of time in her dorm room, reading or watching the Mets on her TV. The relationship went from lightning to showers to drizzle. It died softly the year I was in graduate school and she was in an upstate medical school. The breakup, gentle as it was, established the melancholy of that year, the sense of confusion.

Though we stayed together until after we both graduated, I think I may have realized we wouldn't last sometime during my junior year, the year I discovered poetry—the year I sat with freezing hands trying to record the images of the divestment protests. We rarely argued, but once, in a discussion about our futures, she stated forcefully, "I want a nice house. I want to make money. These things are important to me." She knew I didn't feel the same way. I knew she was being honest. I also knew I could never marry someone with those priorities. Either she would have to change—I couldn't imagine myself changing—or we would have to, eventually, split up. We eventually split up.

Race or class? Race and class? Now I teach Langston Hughes's *Selected Poems*. I've published articles on Hughes and *The Big Sea*, and I reread his autobiography every few years, checking in on his life and mine. With each read, I more plainly hear a voice shaped by the blues—staving off misery through laughter—at oneself, at the world. I get, again and again, a sense that a moral life is easy to understand and to live. One simply need not worry about a nice house, about making money. What is more difficult, nearly impossible, is to be a self in a world that views things so differently from you.

At the end of the 1986–87 school year, all Columbia University English master's candidates had to take an exam. The exam scores, coupled with grades on the two master's essays that we had to write, were the main factors in determining whether one was accepted into the doctoral program or given a master's and simply dismissed. A chart was taped to the door of the graduate office with Social Security numbers, exam scores, and then, in the final column, a Y or an N.

In Philosophy Hall, I walked up the stairs in terror, hardly able to lift my feet. My mouth was dry. An acquaintance walked by me and I managed a weak "Heh," which was supposed to mean "Hi."

There was my number, there were my scores—a bit lower than I'd hoped, but OK—and there was the letter: N. I double-checked it.

Had I read the wrong line? I drew my finger across the page, from my number to the N. Then, I scanned the other grades, the Ys and the Ns. It was clear that I was borderline. Some with worse scores had been accepted, a few with my scores had been rejected.

It was nothing personal. Indeed, that was exactly the point. There was nothing personal from my year there: the cocktail parties I'd slipped in and out of—eating and drinking more than speaking—the seminar classes that I doodled my way through, unsure what to make of other students actually speaking. I had been unprepared for graduate school. I never realized that I was expected to do the secondary reading. Yet Columbia was unprepared for me as well. No one knew how to approach me, to recognize my discomfort with wine and cheese, my puzzlement over why I felt so drawn to walking the streets and riding the subways of New York. Borderline suburban but unversed in the subtleties of class and culture, fundamentally uncertain of whether I deserved to be in this place, or wanted to be in it, I was answered with an N.

There is a loneliness in New York, a beautiful loneliness, beautiful in that it is shared. It is common, like the subways, coursing underneath, surfacing occasionally in a blur of color and sound and fury. That school year of 1986–87, when my baseball friends had gone, when my girlfriend had gone, when Columbia seemed expensive and purposeless, when I'd take the train home nearly every weekend and crash in my parents' house, watch TV and write poems long after they had gone to bed. . . . I couldn't play life as a game anymore. Those numberless, nameless people on New York's streets, their faces all colors, their voices profane and poetic at once—if I was anyone at all, I was one of them. And who were they? Those people Langston Hughes had just dropped himself into—splash!—like a book falling into the sea.

Is this any more or less true than class, or race? It is part of the same story of what keeps us apart, what keeps us tying each other in garbage bags and covering each other in shit, or, worse, doing it to ourselves.

> Sometimes perhaps, you don't want to be a part of me.
> Nor do I often want to be a part of you.
> But we are, that's true!

What's true? I may not have gotten the teaching job I have today without that "Columbia University" on my vitae. Salem State's core curriculum resembles Columbia's with its emphasis on classics.

What's true? Tawana Brawley? The evidence points to a fabricated story by a teen frightened by an abusive stepfather that, in the hands of ambitious lawyers, became a racial flashpoint. Then again, Tawana herself has never spoken about the case under oath. So who knows? The "race riot" at Columbia? Was it unsafe to enter Morningside Park as a white person? Who knows?

Hughes went on to travel the world—Africa, the Soviet Union, the Caribbean, Paris. He wrote and wrote and wrote, poems, plays, short stories, autobiographies, musicals, newspaper columns. He was the first African American to make a living solely on his writing, a life choice that still astonishes for its boldness. Despite a few heterosexual affairs in his twenties and several suspected homosexual affairs, he never had a single long-time lover, never married. His was a lonely life.

I'm thirty-eight and have been to Canada. I've never crossed an ocean, never tossed my books into the waves. I go to library book sales and bring home boxes of books I'll never read. I've got two degrees from Columbia, and two more from Indiana University. I'm married, with two boys, grounded with tenure in one of the oldest cities of the New World. My ancestors were Greek and British, my descendants will be Irish and German, too. This is my theme for English B.

WHAT ONE KNOWS: AN APPRECIATION

Late afternoon, the fifth-floor hallway nearly empty. Far down the corridor, there's one door ajar, the rest of the faculty offices sealed behind opaque yellow windows. My professor, John Eakin, unlocks his door, and the two of us step inside, then sit, he in a swivel chair, and I in a hard wooden one. My backpack thuds on the tiles. Over his left shoulder are rows of autobiographies and scholarly books on autobiography. He brings his hands up in front of his chest and presses his fingers against each other, making a see-through pyramid. His slack hair parts to the left; short, but somehow not neat, a few strands escaping. Glasses, a thin face.

"I'm worried about my paper." A twenty-five-page seminar paper was due in less than two weeks. I'd turned in an eight-page proposal, with an outline and annotated bibliography, and it had been harshly and accurately critiqued by the class the day before.

It was spring semester, my first year in graduate school at Indiana University. I considered myself a poet—I was getting a Master's degree in Fine Arts—but I was taking a literature seminar on autobiography, Eakin's specialty. Before the semester began, I had called him to ask whether I could take the class; I was a creative writer, after all, with only a side interest in his field. He said he'd be happy to have me.

It was an afternoon class, one that, at the beginning of the semester, adjourned just as dusk descended over the campus. The light, despite the wall of windows, always seemed stale. Six of us crowded around one end of the long table. Even for a seminar room, it felt empty.

The first class, he had tried to encourage discussion, but he would get carried away, speaking animatedly, thin arms contorting into oblique angles, rising from his chair and scrawling ideas on the board in complex diagrams. To me, it was often incomprehensible, but he was so earnest and energetic that I felt I just needed to try harder.

The reading list, like the man, was eclectic, ranging from St. Augustine to Lillian Hellman, and the class had become a refreshing break from the intensive creative work I was doing. For the past few days, though, I had been deeply regretting enrolling in it. I knew that my plan for the paper was weak, and now, embarrassingly, the class knew it, too. I was used to harsh critiques in poetry workshops and was able to dismiss those because of my brash, unjustified confidence in my own poems. Yet I had little faith in my scholarship. I was haunted by the dismal year I'd spent in Columbia's English master's program. The words of one of the faculty readers for my master's essay still fueled self-doubt. He had called my language "enervating" and quoted a passage to underscore his point, introducing it with, "Listen to this one: . . ."

I'm worried about my paper.

Eakin was leaning back in his chair, his fingers still pressing into each other.

"Frankly, I'm worried, too," he said, simply. It was not a response that I expected. It was not an awkward evasion, tinged with pity and condescension. He did not exaggerate the few positives and make me feel that some tinkering would suffice. And yet it was not a cruel response. He didn't emphasize his expertise and my ignorance.

He was *worried*, about *me*. And he was willing to tell me so. We were both worried; we were in this together. He summarized the criticisms that I'd heard, crystallizing my problems. He did not do it discouragingly, yet he did not do it encouragingly. He was showing me the obstacles ahead. How I would deal with them was up to me.

I left the office a few minutes later, neither crestfallen nor buoyed but focused, and weary—anticipating all the work to be done. Late that week, on Friday afternoon, I slipped a revised draft of the proposal into his mailbox at school. The next morning, after another night of writing, I was awakened by the phone. I crawled out of my narrow dorm bed and opened the wooden cabinet in the wall that housed the swiveling phone I shared with my neighbor. It was Mr. Eakin, calling to tell me that the proposal now looked good. He had one or two pertinent questions, but on the whole it was much clearer than before. I hung up the phone and, rather than going back to bed, took a few enthusiastic hops, then clicked on my computer to continue working.

As I waited for the computer to start up, I thought of Eakin and the effort that he had made: at the end of the work week, finding some pages of a desperate student in his box, and spending his Friday evening reading, assessing. He had worked around any plans he may have made—time with his family, his own reading and writing. He must have recognized *my* effort, and the phone call was his way of letting me know that—it was an assertion of quiet, firm faith. I did fine on that paper, and I went on to get a doctorate in American literature. I wrote my dissertation on autobiography, with John Eakin as my advisor.

———

I still refer to him as Mr. Eakin, except to his face. He'd asked that I call him John as we shook hands after lunch a few weeks after the seminar had ended. Now, I can almost do it without thinking, but for a long time, it seemed unnatural, a slight. And yet, why do I write about him as a teacher when his advice to a graduate student about teaching was, *teach with your left hand?*

Like all good teachers, he taught by example. He freed me as a
student because he freed himself from the debilitating notion of
college professor as all knowing. Once, in a conversation about
graduate exams, he confessed to not having read a book, some clas-
sic of Dickens (*me, too!* my mind shouted). In that first seminar, as
we were struggling through a passage, he made a liberating, frank
admission: "I confess," he said, "that there are times when I find this
essay impenetrable" (*me too!*). Another time, over lunch, he told of
a conversation with a younger colleague who had asked for a cri-
tique of his work. When Eakin had commented that the writing felt
"dense," the author had responded, "But I like that. I like the dense
style." Telling the story, Eakin shrugged and chuckled bemusedly.

But these admissions are not celebrations of ignorance. Eakin
is one of the most respected scholars in his field. At a National
Endowment for the Humanities seminar that I attended, he came
in to give a guest lecture, and he was introduced as Mr. Autobiography. He has been a keynote speaker at international conferences
and has published some of the most influential, most cited books
in life-writing. Occasionally, my eyes became bleary trying to read
them. His own writing can be difficult, but it is generally clearer and
more readable than the essays he assigned.

Despite his stature, Eakin retained an openness to learning. One
semester I served as a teaching assistant for his nineteenth-century
American literature class—150 students in an echoing hall, he generally lecturing, asking the occasional question. When the other TA
and I team-taught one class, Eakin sat in the audience, a few rows
back. Working off notes but speaking informally, we led the class
through some Hawthorne stories. Unlike Eakin, we elicited student
questions and comments, and built our ideas on them.

Eakin listened, fully engaged, and waved his hand a few times
to add comments. He swiveled his neck, noting the liveliness of

the class, the students raising their hands, commenting, laughing. Afterward, he told us that he'd been inspired, and the next class he departed from a set lecture and stepped out from behind the podium, even called on a few students.

Teach with your left hand. We should save our real, best effort for ourselves, our own work. What useful, memorable advice to the unfocused graduate student! But what now, now that I'm at a college that emphasizes teaching, now that teaching, as much as writing, gives me deep satisfaction? What if one is, like me, left-handed?

I have learned from John that true teaching only occurs organically, even accidentally. Like writing, one stumbles upon moments of connection, moments that might help shape a life. The most valuable, lasting lessons from a class are almost never the teacher's main points. Some flip comment crystallizes into astonishing truth in the student's mind. The teacher may never know.

At the time I was to take my graduate exams, Indiana University was instituting a new process. In order to help students prepare for their dissertations, the exams no longer aimed to be comprehensive, but focused on the individual student's research interests; in fact, some advisors allowed the student to construct the reading list, and even the exam itself. The guidelines were vague, which caused confusion; some advisors and committees were encouraging student input, while others were demanding students still prepare for more broad-based exams.

Eakin encouraged me to develop my own question. "It's easy to find out what someone doesn't know," he explained to my committee. The implication: it was harder to discover what knowledge and perspective someone did offer, and that a teacher's charge was to help the student make such discoveries. Only gradually has the full wisdom of his statement become clear, only gradually have I assimilated it into not only my teaching, but my life. Each person has something to teach, each person can learn from himself. They just might need a little help seeing how.

In this era of tests and accountability in education, when raising scores is the mark of educational success, John's idea establishes a different, bolder standard of educational rigor. If you get your working-class students to answer one more question right on a standardized test, you will have turned them into middle-class students. Congratulations. But will they remember any words that you have said, will they take them home and carry them for years, your sentences helping to shape their sentences, their world? Will they remember you, the way I will reminisce about John years from now, still referring to him, respectfully, as Mr. Eakin?

NOT LIKE ME (AN EXERCISE)

In the first poetry class I took at Columbia, my teacher suggested an exercise: Write a poem that is a lie. How I hated that! It went against all of what I, just beginning to write, believed poetry to be—noble, profound, and true. She wanted me to imagine that the moon really was made of cheese (this was one of her examples). I wanted to write about my family. In rebellion, I wrote "Two Lies about My Family." Here is the first section:

When My Brother Died

My behind-the-back passes roll
into neighbors' gardens. My aggressive
fighting for rebounds goes unchallenged.
My headfakes fool only people watching
through windows whispering, "He's supposed
to be a smart Columbia boy."

The ball bouncing all night on the pavement
annoys everyone—even my parents
sitting at the kitchen table, drinking coffee,
and my sister, locked silent in her room,
with the old box of photos and clippings.

The pounded ball grows hard and smooth
like a boulder in the sea, a boulder
that has been on this earth too long.

What follows is an act of imagined autobiography.

He seems like a student I will easily forget. He's silent in class, and, though he doesn't fall asleep, I notice that he doodles more than he takes notes. Once, I thought I made out the word *Sleep* in block letters across the top of one of his notebook pages, another time I thought I saw *Nomar* and *Manny* with some numbers (their stats?) beside them.

He's usually already sitting in the class when I arrive, but he's rarely talking to the other students. Sometimes he just listens to their conversations. Sometimes he'll have his book open, reading, with a hint of desperation, the essay that was on the syllabus for the day. When the class starts, he closes the book, and opens his notebook.

Like many of my students, he seems like he doesn't care much about his grade. He makes very little effort to participate in class, and, although he turns in competent work on time, his early assignments are uninspired. Once, I asked my class to eavesdrop on a conversation and transcribe it. It was a way for them to discover the freshness within ordinary speech. His dialogue read like bad Beckett:

MAN #1: What's up?
MAN #2: Nothin'. You?
MAN #1: Just hangin'. Got class in ten minutes.
MAN #2: With Reynolds?
MAN #1: Yeah.

He's rather pathetic, really, with his bumpy heavy acne. I notice his fingers rubbing and pinching his face, and have an urge to tell him to stop. His hair is parted in the middle, a plain look, like a high school athlete, or a fast-food worker. It's not like mine, which is parted, a bit vaguely, to the side. I used to part my hair in the middle, before I began teaching college and grew a moustache. I was twenty-two, and I needed to look older, to establish some distance from those seated in front of me. A part to the side, a moustache, and voilà, I was a professor, or at least an instructor—"How old are you?" one of my students asked during that first semester.

"How old do you think I am?"

"Twenty-seven."

"That's about right."

He's short, too, though he does seem in shape, lithe. The way he moves into and out of the classroom is smooth, almost studied. His walk reminds me of basketball, loose yet deliberate.

I wish I could feel for him more. I could, if he didn't seem so unenthusiastic. It's frustrating to notice him gazing vaguely at his nearly blank notebook, clearly not listening. He only revealed energy when I took attendance the first day and called him John.

"I go by J.," he said.

"Jay?"

"Yeah. J-period."

That name meant a lot to him, apparently. He seemed to care more about that than any writing, or reading, we would do in class.

When I break the class into small groups, J. remains quiet, although he occasionally makes statements of fact about the readings—useful statements that correct a misperception that had sprouted up among the louder members of the group: Maxine Hong Kingston never lived in China. She was imagining what her aunt's life was like. He offers these observations tentatively, "I thought that it said . . ." or "I might be wrong, but . . ." His comments are tangled with *maybe's* and *I don't know's*.

When we discuss James Baldwin's "Notes of a Native Son," I notice that, as usual, he isn't following the conversation, but he is engrossed. I step to the center of the class circle and sneak a glimpse, see what has put him in this state: slack jawed, body poised yet relaxed, an athlete's concentration. It is Baldwin's words. He is rapt in the reading that he was supposed to have done before class, his intensity so visible that I want to ask him which page he's on.

I'm not angered by his inattention. Baldwin's words are more exciting than anything we have to say about them. Well, that's something, I think. That's something.

When he turned in his second paper, things changed. In my composition classes, I have my students read essays by Baldwin, Kingston, and others, and then give them this assignment:

> Write a portrait of a human being who has bewildered, haunted, frustrated, or angered you. It can be a close friend, a relative, an enemy, or someone that you don't know well, but have always been curious about. Try to reach an understanding of that person by considering his/her history, as Baldwin does with his father, and as Kingston does with her aunt. What were some of the circumstances of the person's life that help shed light on who the person became? You might consider significant details about the person's family or community as a way of explaining the person (as Kingston and Baldwin do). You might want to focus on one incident in the person's life that helps you, and us, understand that person better (as Kingston does). You might also incorporate how this person's life story is related to your own.

J. wrote a paper about his brother's death. This wasn't unusual. Many students write about someone they cared about who died, but J.'s paper didn't follow the predictable pattern. He focused not on the traumatic moment of death, or the funeral, but on the months after. And he didn't conclude that the experience has led him to "appreciate every day" or to "be all that he can be." In fact, I can't remember what his conclusion was. Whatever it was, it wasn't important. (What philosophy can nineteen-year-olds really offer? Or, for that mat-

ter, thirty-eight-year-olds?) What remains with me is the image of
him playing basketball by himself on a winter night in his family's
driveway after shoveling off the snow, skeins of ice in the cement's
dips, fingers, as he put it, "red, raw, almost numb. My right pinkie
is throbbing and hot because it has broken a few times and the
circulation is messed up. In the faint, pale glow from the light over
the garage door, I almost can see my brother, cutting to the basket,
or even rushing at me, his knees bending to leap and try and block
my shot. I fake, though no one is there, and let his ghost sail past,
then drive hard to the hoop as if I could jump high enough to jam
one home."

"Great," I'd written in the margins. "You are a writer!"

It is a perverse fact that one way to stop Salem State students from
coming to class is to praise their work. I'll call students aside to
encourage them to become English majors, and, almost inevitably,
they will start missing classes. Some show up a few more times, then
stop coming altogether. I never spoke to J. about his paper, but my
enthusiasm shone through my comments, and, soon, he started
missing a class a week, usually Thursday. His next paper was well
done, a character analysis of a piece of literature, but I was getting
frustrated. He wasn't *that* smart. He could be learning things, if
only he'd come.

One day, mid-April, he does come—not to class, but to office
hours. A knock on my open door as I'm reading my e-mail. I swivel
around. He's standing outside the office in sweatpants and a baseball
cap. He looks healthy, tan, his acne dried out by the sun. "Hi," he
says, "can I talk to you?"

I gesture to the chair wedged against my filing cabinet. "Sure. Sit
down. Sit down." He sits, setting his backpack at his feet.

"I'm worried about my grade. I know I've missed some classes.
Am I going to pass?"

I open my beat-up grade book, the taped cover half off the rings, and scan the row of X's and blank rectangles. Seven absences. "You've missed quite a few."

"I'm on the baseball team. We've had games the last few Thursdays, and the bus leaves at 1:15. There's only one more game."

"I wish you had told me earlier. We could have made arrangements."

"I'm sorry." He seems sorry. He seems to be bracing for punishment. Will I make him drop the class? Insist he quit baseball?

"What position do you play?" I ask.

His head moves a notch. He hadn't expected me to say that. "Outfield. Some center, usually left."

"I used to play."

He's silent, then "uh-huh."

"Well," I say, "your grade will take a hit. But you're a good writer. If you come to class from here on out, you'll be OK."

"Oh, good," he says. "Thanks." He bends to pick up his backpack, and I notice the pinkie on his right hand. It's swollen at the joint, and the top half angles out, away from the other fingers.

"You know, I've got to tell you—" I start. He lets go of the backpack and looks up, a bit fearfully, "that last essay of yours was really moving. Very powerful."

I think I see a smile about to break out, but then he steadies himself, offers a noncommittal, "thanks." I watch him studying the titles in my bookcase, the row of alphabetized poetry books behind my head.

"I'm sorry about your brother," I say.

He nods. "Yeah, that was hard."

"I can imagine."

"I wasn't going to come here," he says. "I was going to Columbia, in New York City." He says this like it's a question, as if asking whether I had heard of Columbia. I nod.

"But things got so crazy when he died. I didn't even want to go to college. I took a year off, ended up here."

I want to hear more. "Are you an English major?"

"No, math."

"I didn't realize we actually had math majors here." I smile. He smiles back politely.

"You should think about being an English major, or at least take some writing classes." Pause.

"Have you enjoyed writing?"

"Yeah."

"What about reading? Have you liked any of the essays I've had you read?"

"I liked that one about the father," he says.

"'Notes of a Native Son'? James Baldwin?"

"Yeah, I liked how he wrote about his family, but also about all that other stuff—the war, the race riots . . ."

"It's one of my—"

"And that one . . ."—he's talking! I've learned to shut up in these moments—"the story that everyone said was boring, 'I'm standing here ironing.'"

"'I Stand Here Ironing.' Tillie Olsen."

"I stand here ironing," he says. "It was . . ."

"I've always had a soft spot for that story," I pause. Does he need to hear my story? Do I need to tell it? He's looking at me—intently, I think, or at least intently for him. So much for him talking. I go on.

"One day when my wife and I were in grad school, we were just lying around on the sofa. I don't know why, but I decided to read aloud to her as she rested on me, her head on my chest." I tap my chest. "So I began reading 'I Stand Here Ironing.' When I got to the last page, I kept having to stop and regain my composure, to catch myself from weeping. I staggered to the finish, choking up every few sentences, then looked and saw that my wife was crying, too. It was an amazing moment." He offers a vague smile and shifts in his chair.

I leap up, reach over the filing cabinet, and pull down the reader from the bookcase beside him. I flip the pages, mumbling "amazing." I find the last paragraphs, where the unnamed working-class mother completes her musing over the note that she has received from her daughter's college counselor. The counselor feels the daughter, Emily, "needs help" and hopes to talk with the mother about her. Usually, in class, I read quickly, but today, in this quiet office, I read deliberately. As I read, many of my students come to mind, too many—the mother who lost her husband early and was trying to stay enrolled, but at last couldn't afford it. The woman who had been abused by her father, who dropped in and out of school. The woman interested in being a writer, but who, with two young children, only had time and money for one course a year. The man who had grown up in the projects; at thirty-six, he suffered a serious motorcycle accident, then decided to come to college. He said to me, "I just wish I had done this a lot earlier." He was my age. And this young man in front of me—a boy, really—who has lost his best friend, his brother. All of them talented, all of them scarred.

I read, and the mother's voice seems infinitely wiser than mine:

"I will never total it all. I will never come in to say: She was a child seldom smiled at. Her father left me before she was a year old. I had to work her first six years when there was work, or I sent her home and to his relatives. There were years she had care she hated. She was dark and thin and foreign looking in a world where the prestige went to blondeness and curly hair and dimples, she was slow where glibness was prized. She was a child of anxious, not proud, love. We were poor and could not afford for her the soil of easy growth. I was a young mother, I was a distracted mother. There were other children pushing up, demanding. Her younger sister seemed all that she was not. There were years she did not want me to touch her. She kept too much in herself, her life was such that she had to keep too much in herself. My wisdom came too late. She has much to her and probably little will come of it—"

I pause, catch my breath, and wipe my face with my forearm. A tear drops onto the sleeve of my sweater. "Jesus," I say, looking up and laughing. "It's happening again." J. is staring at me—in horror? In wonder? I've never cried in front of a student before. "Oh, screw it," I say. "I might as well finish," and I do:

". . . She is a child of her age, of depression, of war, of fear.

"Let her be. So all that is in her will not bloom—but in how many does it? There is still enough left to live by. Only help her to know—help make it so there is cause for her to know—that she is more than this dress on the ironing board, helpless before the iron."

I can't tell how he feels about what I've just read, just done. He looks at me a few moments as if he wants to study my face—the missed hairs from shaving blind in the shower, the slight bend in my once-broken nose from an elbow during a game of hoops. Then his eyes drop to his hands in his lap.

I don't know if he'll ever graduate. He's still trying to make peace with his brother's death. I don't know if he's reachable or not. Did he understand what Olsen was trying to say, what I was trying to tell him?

What was I trying to tell him?

Whatever his response, he will remember this moment, remember *me*. At some time, several years from now, he'll recall how his freshman composition teacher wept in front of him telling a story about his own life. He may share the story with others—friends, lovers, even students. I cannot say what he will make of it, whether he will use it as an example of weakness, or self-absorption, or learning.

If this were fiction, the story would end here. But, of course, I close the book and compose myself, and, some barriers broken, we chat a bit. As I am going on, circling an abstract point, my head tilts upward, to the left, and my eye catches on the tree limbs outside my window, the network of branches, buds just thick enough now to be visible from where I sit. Soon they will bloom small white tear-shaped petals that will obscure the power plant's smokestacks on the other side of town. Soon, the leaves will mottle the blue sky, and their shadows will mottle the pavement and cracked steps below. In my bones, I feel the oncoming summer, and I imagine playing baseball with my sons down at the park they call "train park" because it's across the river from Salem's commuter rail stop. I'm on the mound, forty-five feet away, and toss pitch after pitch, just like I did with my own, still-very-much-alive brother in our family's Connecticut backyard when we were teenagers. The boys swing and swing and swing, and I make observations: "Don't pull off the ball." "Keep your elbow up." The surge of joy when one of them connects and the ball shoots into the outfield or rises high into the windy air, sailing over the head of the other, the one in the gooseshit-scarred dirt.

My own life calls to me, and I shut up.

"OK?" I say, as if I have explained everything.

WHY ARE WE EVEN HERE FOR?

As a teacher of writing and literature at Salem State College, I hear a lot of stories. My students, although they may never have ventured more than twenty miles from where they were born, bring hard lessons of endurance to the classroom that seem more profound than any I'd had at their age. For years I've believed that they bring a certain wisdom to the class, a wisdom that doesn't score on the SAT or other standardized tests. The old teaching cliché—I learn from my students—feels true, but it is hard to explain. I'm not particularly naive. I know that life can be difficult. So it is not that my students initiate me into the world of sorrow. It is that they often bring their sorrows, and their struggles, to the material, and when they do, it makes life and literature seem so entwined as to be inseparable.

This past year, for the first time, I taught African American literature: two sections each semester of a yearlong sequence, around twenty-two students per section. The first semester we began with Phyllis Wheatley and ended with the Harlem Renaissance. The second semester we started with Zora Neale Hurston and Richard Wright and ended with Percival Everett's satire, *Erasure*, published early in the new millennium.

The students in these classes weren't the ones I typically had in my writing classes. About half were white, and the other half were black, Latino, or Asian. They were generally uninterested or inexperienced in reading, simply trying to satisfy the college's literature requirement. One day before spring break I was assigning the class a hundred pages from Toni Morrison's *Sula*, and one student looked aghast. "We have to read during vacation?" he sputtered.

I learned from them the whole year.

In the fall semester, I was teaching W. E. B. Du Bois's *The Souls of Black Folk*. As classes go, it had been fairly dull. Du Bois's essays didn't have the compelling story line of the slave narratives that we had read earlier in the semester. We had just begun examining Du Bois's idea of "double-consciousness." It is a complicated notion that an African American, at least around 1900 when Du Bois was writing, had "no true self-consciousness" because he was "always looking at one's self through the eyes of others, . . . measuring one's soul by the tape of a world that looks on in amused contempt and pity." In class, I read this definition, paraphrased it, then asked, "Does this make sense to you?"

There was the usual pause after I ask a question and then, from Omar, a large, seemingly lethargic African American, came a soulful, deep-throated "yeah." The word reverberated in the haphazard circle of desks as we registered the depths from which he had spoken. The room's silence after his "yeah" was not the bored silence that had preceded it. The air was charged. Someone had actually meant something he had said. Someone was talking about his own life, even if it was only one word.

I followed up: "So what do you do about this feeling? How do you deal with it?"

Everyone was staring at Omar, but he didn't seem to notice. He looked at me a second, then put his head down and shook it, slowly, as if seeing and thinking were too much for him. "I don't know, man. I don't know."

The rest of the heads in class dropped down, too, and students began reviewing the passage, which was no longer just a bunch of incomprehensible words by some long-dead guy with too many initials.

Every book that we studied after that day, some student would bring up double-consciousness, incorporating it smartly into our discussion. Omar had branded the concept into everyone's minds, including mine.

One idea that arises from double consciousness is that, without a "true self-consciousness," you risk giving in and accepting society's definitions of yourself, becoming what society tells you that you are. Such a capitulation may be what happens to Bigger Thomas, the protagonist of Richard Wright's *Native Son*, a novel we read during the second semester. *Native Son* is a brutal book. Bigger, a poor African American from the Chicago ghetto, shows little regret after he murders two women. His first victim is Mary, the daughter of a wealthy white family for whom Bigger works as a driver. After Bigger carries a drunk, semiconscious Mary up to her room, he accidentally suffocates her with a pillow while trying to keep her quiet so his presence won't be discovered. Realizing what he has done, he hacks up her body and throws it in the furnace. Emboldened rather than horrified, he writes a ransom note to the family and eventually kills his girlfriend, Bessie, whom he drags into the scheme. In the end, he's found out, and, after Chicago is thrown into a hysterical, racist-charged panic, he's caught, brought to trial—a very long trial that contains a communist lawyer's exhaustive defense of Bigger that is an indictment of capitalism and racism—and sentenced to death.

Readers, to this day, are not sure what to make of Bigger. Is he to be pitied? Is he a warning? A symbol? A product of American racism?

During the second week of teaching *Native Son*, I was walking through the college's athletic facility when I heard my name, "Mr. Scrimgeour. Mr. Scrimgeour . . ."

I turn and it is Keith, an African American from the class. "Hey, I wanted to tell you, I'm sorry."

"Sorry?" He has missed a few classes, but no more than most students. Maybe he hasn't turned in his last response paper.

"Yeah, I'm going to talk in class more." I nod. He looks at me as if I'm not following. "Like Bigger, I don't know . . . I don't like it." His white baseball cap casts a shadow over his face so that I can barely see his eyes.

"What don't you like?"

"He's, like," Keith grimaces, as if he isn't sure that he should say what he is about to say. "He's like a stereotype—he's like what people—some people—say about us."

On "us," he points to his chest, takes a step back, and gives a pained half grin, his teeth a bright contrast to his dark, nearly black skin.

"Yeah," I say. "That's understandable. You should bring that up in the next class. We'll see what other people think."

He nods. "And I'm sorry, " he says, taking another step back, "It's just that. . . ." He taps his chest again, "I'm shy."

Keith has trouble forming complete sentences when he writes. I don't doubt that my fourth-grade son can write with fewer grammatical errors. Yet he had identified the criticism of Wright's book made by such writers as James Baldwin and David Bradley, whose essays on *Native Son* we would read after we finished the novel. And he knew something serious was at stake—his life—that chest, and what was inside it, that he'd tapped so expressively. Was Bigger what Baldwin identified as the "inverse" of the saccharine Uncle Tom stereotype? Was Wright denying Bigger humanity? And, if so, should we be reading the book?

To begin answering these questions required an understanding of Bigger. For me, such an understanding would come not just from the text, but from my students' own lives.

That Keith apologized for his lack of participation in class is not surprising. My students are generally apologetic. "I'm so ashamed," one student said to me, explaining why she didn't get a phone message I'd left her. "I live in a shelter with my daughter." Many of them feel a sense of guilt for who they are, a sense that whatever went wrong must be their fault. These feelings, while often debilitating, enable my students, even Keith, to understand Bigger, perhaps better than most critics. Keith, who—at my prompting—spoke in class about being pulled over by the police, understood the accumulation of guilt that makes you certain that what you are doing, and what you will do, is wrong. Bigger says he knew he was going to murder someone long before he actually does, that it was as if he had already murdered.

Unlike his critics, Richard Wright had an unrelentingly negative upbringing. As he details in his autobiography, *Black Boy*, Wright was raised in poverty by a family that discouraged books in the violently racist South. There was little, if anything, that was sustaining or nurturing. Perhaps a person has to have this sense of worthlessness ground into one's life to conceive of a character like Bigger. Like my students, one must be told that one isn't much often enough so that it is not simply an insult, but a seemingly intractable truth.

"I'm sorry," Keith had said. It was something Bigger could never really bring himself to say, and in this sense the Salem State students were much different from Bigger. Their response to society's intimidation isn't Bigger's rebelliousness. Wright documents Bigger's sense of discomfort in most social interactions, particularly when speaking with whites, during which he is rendered virtually mute, stumbling through "yes, sirs" and loathing both himself and the whites while doing so.

Although my students weren't violent, they identified with Bigger's discomfort—they'd experienced similar, less extreme discomforts talking to teachers, policemen, and other authority figures. As a way into discussing Bigger, I'd asked them to write for a few minutes in class about a time in which they felt uncomfortable and how they had responded to the situation. I joined them in the exercise. Here's what I wrote:

> As a teenager, after school, I would go with a few other guys and smoke pot in the parking lot of the local supermarket, then go into the market's foyer and play video games stoned. While I felt uncomfortable about smoking pot in the parking lot, I didn't really do much. I tried to urge the guys I was with to leave the car and go inside and play the video games, but it wouldn't mean the same thing: to just go in and play the games would be childish, uncool, but to do it after smoking pot made it o.k.—and once I was in the foyer, it was o.k.; I wouldn't get in trouble.
>
> But mostly I did nothing to stop us. I toked, like everyone else. I got quiet. I didn't really hear the jokes, but forced laughter anyway. I was very attentive to my surroundings—was that lady walking out with the grocery cart looking at us? Afterward, when we went in and manipulated those electronic pulses of light and laughed at our failures, we weren't just laughing at our failures, we were laughing at what we had gotten away with.

After they had worked in groups, comparing their own experiences to Bigger's, I shared my own writing with the class. Of course, there were smiles, as well as a few looks of astonishment and approbation. I had weighed whether to confess to my "crime," and determined that it might lead to learning, as self-disclosure can sometimes do, and so here I was, hanging my former self out on a laundry line for their inspection.

What came of the discussion was, first of all, how noticeable the differences were between my experience and Bigger's. I was a middle-class white boy who assumed he would be going to college. I believed I had a lot to lose from being caught, while Bigger, trapped in a life of poverty, may not have felt such risks. Also, the discomfort I was feeling was from peer pressure, rather than from the dominant power structure. Indeed, my discomfort arose from the fact that I was breaking the rules, whereas Bigger's arose from trying to follow the rules—how he was supposed to act around whites.

But there was also a curious similarity between my experience and Bigger's. Playing those video games would have meant something different had we not smoked pot beforehand. The joy of wasting an afternoon dropping quarters into Galaga was about knowing that we had put one over on the authorities; it was about the thrill of getting away with something, of believing, for at least a brief time, that we were immune to society's rules. Like me after I was safely in the supermarket, Bigger, upon seeing that he could get away with killing Mary, felt "a queer sense of power," and believed that he was "living, truly and deeply." In a powerless life, Bigger had finally tasted the possibility of power.

My students know Bigger moderately well. They don't have his violent streak; they don't know his feelings of being an outsider, estranged from family and community despite hanging out with his cronies in the pool hall and being wept over by his mother.

What they understand is his sense of powerlessness. They have never been told that they can be players on the world stage, and, mostly, their lives tell them that they can't, whether it's the boss who (they think) won't give them one night off a semester to go to a poetry reading, or the anonymous authority of the education-al bureaucracy that tells them that due to a missed payment, or deadline, they are no longer enrolled. As one student writes in his midterm: "Bigger is an African American man living in a world where who he is and what he does doesn't matter, and in his mind never will."

I went to a talk recently by an elderly man who had worked for the CIA for thirty years, an engineer involved with nuclear submarines who engaged in the cloak-and-dagger of the cold war. The layers of secrecy astonish. How much was going on under the surface!—the trailing and salvaging of nuclear subs; the alerts in which cities and nations were held over the abyss in the trembling fingers of men as lost as the rest of us, though they generally did not realize it.

During the questions afterward, someone asked about the massive buildup of nuclear arsenals. "Didn't anyone look at these thousands of nuclear warheads we were making and say, 'This is crazy'?"

The speaker nodded, his bald, freckled head moving slowly. He took a deep breath. "It was crazy, but when you are in the middle of it, it is hard to see. No one said anything."

After the talk, I fell into conversation with the speaker's son, a psychologist in training. I was noting how tremendously distant this world of espionage was from the world of my students, how alien it was. And I said that the stories of near nuclear annihilation frightened me a lot more than they would frighten them. In essence, my students saw their lives like Bigger's: The great world of money and power was uninterested in them and moved in its ways regardless of what they did. Like Bigger, they would never fly the airplanes that he, who had once dreamed of being a pilot, watches passing over the Chicago ghetto.

"It's too bad they feel so disempowered," the son said, and it is. Yet there is something valuable in their psychology, too. It is liberating to let that world—money and power—go, to be able to see the outlines of your existence, so that you can begin to observe, and know, and ultimately make an acceptable marriage with your life. Some might say it is the first step to becoming a writer.

After September 11, 2001, a surprising number of students didn't exhibit the depth of horror that I had witnessed others display on television. "I'm sorry if I sound cold," one student said, "but that has nothing to do with me." One of my most talented students even wrote in an essay, "The war has nothing to do with my life. I mean the blood and the death disgusts me, but I'm sorry—I just don't care."

And then I watched them realize how it did indeed have to do with them. It meant that they lost their jobs at the airport, or they got called up and sent to Afghanistan or Iraq. The world doesn't let you escape that easily. Bigger got the chair.

It has been two months since we finished *Native Son*. The school year is ending, and I rush to class, a bit late, trying to decide whether to cancel it so that I can have lunch with a job candidate—we're hiring someone in multicultural literature, and I'm on the search committee. As I make my way over, I feel the tug of obligation—my students would benefit from a discussion of the ending of Percival Everett's *Erasure*, even though, or perhaps especially because, almost none of them have read it. Yet it's a fine spring day, a Friday, and they will not be interested in being in class, regardless of what I pull out of my teaching bag of tricks. I weigh the options—dull class for everyone or the guilt of canceling a class (despite the department chair's suggestion that I cancel it). Before I enter the room, I'm still not quite sure, but I'm leaning toward canceling. I take a deep breath and then breathe out, exhaling my guilt into the tiled hallway.

I open the door; the students are mostly there, sitting in a circle, as usual. Only a few are talking. I walk toward the board, and—I freeze—scrawled across it is:

Why are we even <u>here</u> for?
You already gave us the final.
It's not like you're going to help us answer it.

Looking at it now, I think the underline was a nice touch, but at that moment, for a rage-filled second, I think, "We're going to have class, dammit! Make them suffer." I stand with my back to them, slowing my breath, my options zipping through my mind while sorrow (despair?) and anger bubble in me and pop, pop into the afternoon's clear light.

So much for learning. Were our conversations simply for grades? Was that the real story of this year?

When we discussed *Native Son*, we talked about how easy it was to transfer feelings of guilt to rage at those who make you feel guilty. Bigger's hatred of whites stems from how they make him feel. He pulls a gun and threatens Mary's boyfriend, Jan, when Jan is trying to help him, because Jan has made him feel he has done wrong. In the book, Wright suggests that white society loathes blacks because they are reminders of the great sin of slavery. Is my rage from guilt—guilt that we haven't really accomplished much this year, guilt that I was willing to cancel a class because I didn't want to endure forty-five minutes of bored faces? Pop . . . pop.

I dismiss the class and stroll over to the dining commons to collect my free lunch.

Erasure is a brilliant satire, one that contains an entire novella by the book's protagonist, a frustrated African American writer, Monk Ellison, who has been told one too many times by editors that his writings aren't "black enough." The novel within a novel lifts the plot of *Native Son* almost completely, and it presents a main character, Van Go Jenkins, as the worst stereotype of African American culture, someone without morals, whose only interests are sex and violence. At one point, Van Go slaps one of his sons around—he has four children by four different women—because the mentally handicapped three-year-old spilled juice on Van Go's new shirt.

It's clear that *Erasure*'s narrator, Monk, is appalled by the book he writes, and that he's appalled by *Native Son* and the attitudes about race and writing the novel has fostered. When we do discuss the book in class, I point to a snippet of dialogue that Monk imagines:

D. W. GRIFFITH: I like your book very much.
RICHARD WRIGHT: Thank you.

"So this is a real question *Erasure* raises," I say. My pulse quick-ens. I can sense them listening, waiting. "Is this book right about Richard Wright? Is this book fair to him? To *Native Son*? Has the creation of Bigger Thomas been a disaster for African Americans? Has it skewered the country's view of race in a harmful way?" I pause, content. Even if no one raises a hand, even if no discussion ensues—and certainly some discussion will erupt—I can see the question worming into their minds, a question that they might even try to answer themselves.

La Sauna, the student who never lets me get away with anything, raises her hand: "What do *you* think?"

What do *I* think? I wasn't ready for that. What *do* I think?

What I think, I realize, has been altered by what they think, and what they have taught me about the book, about the world.

There are no definite answers, but my students had helped identify the questions, and had pointed toward possible replies. After we had finished reading *Native Son*, I asked the class, "How many of you want Bigger to get away, even after he bashes in Bessie's head?" A good third of the class raised their hands, and, like the class itself, those who wanted this double murderer to escape were a mix of men and women, blacks and whites. There are several ways to interpret this, but I don't think it is a sign of callousness, the residue of playing too much Grand Theft Auto. They wanted Bigger to escape because Wright had gotten into Bigger's consciousness deeply and believably enough that he became real, more than a symbol or a stereotype.

I tell them this, how their response to Bigger has influenced my reading. I don't tell them Gina's story.

Gina was one of the students who read the books. She loved Tea Cake and Sula, was torn between Martin Luther King Jr. and Malcolm X.

She even visited me in my office once or twice to seek advice about problems with a roommate, or a professor. An African American student from a rough neighborhood, she ended up leaving the college after the semester ended, unable to afford housing costs.

Sometime in March of that semester, Gina came to my office. She had missed class and wanted to turn in her response paper on *Native Son*. The class had read the essays by Baldwin and Bradley criticizing the novel, and had been asked to evaluate them. Baldwin, Gina tells me, was difficult, "but he was such a good writer."

Did she agree with Baldwin, I ask? Was Bigger denied humanity by Wright? How does she feel toward Bigger?

"I think he needs help," she says, "but I felt sorry for him. I wanted him to be able to understand his life—" I cut in, offering some teacherish observation about how Bigger shows glimmers of understanding in the last part of the book, but her mind is far ahead of me, just waiting for me to stop. I do.

"The book reminded me of the guy who killed my uncle. You probably saw it—the trial was all over the TV last week."

I shake my head.

The man and an accomplice had murdered her uncle, a local storeowner, three years ago, and the previous week had been sentenced to life without parole. The two had been friends of the uncle's family, had played pool with the uncle the night before, planning to rob and kill him the next day.

"When I saw him sitting there, with his head down, looking all sad, I don't know, I felt sorry for him. I wanted to give him a copy of *Native Son*. I wanted to walk up to him and put it in his lap. It might help him to understand his life."

She looks at me, her brown face just a few shades darker than mine. She's nineteen. Her hair is pinned back, but some strands float loose. Her eyes are as wide as half dollars, as if she's asking me something. Without thinking, I nod slowly, trying to hold her gaze. On the shelves surrounding us are the papers and books of my profession, that giant horde of words that will pursue me until I die.

"My family wants him to suffer—hard. But I want to talk to him. Do you think that's bad? I want to know why he did it, what happened. I wonder how he'd react if he saw me—what he'd do if I gave him the book."

I imagine *Native Son* in the man's lap. The glossy purple, green, and black cover bright against the courtroom's muted wood, the man's trousers. His hand, smooth with youth, holds its spine. His thumb blots out part of the eerie full-lipped face on the front. As the words of the court fall about him, the book rises and falls ever so slightly, as if breathing.

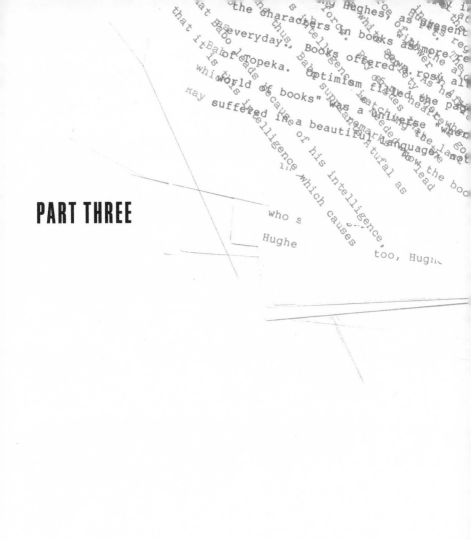

PART THREE

TILTED

It began with a photo. "That's Molly," Caitlin said, "when she went to France last year." Who was Molly? Someone I never knew, but for this—a little gawky, body in angles that seemed absurd to hold, a huge smile, cropped hair, the day looking sunny and fine behind her. While Caitlin called home to check in on her boys, I studied the photo. Molly was clearly happy. She was clearly young. I put it back on Caitlin's desk, beside her keyboard, and looked at the line of photos on the wall of her office. One was of a human triangle, at least a dozen people dressed in flowing white, crammed together, slightly tilted, shaping the outline of what seemed a gigantic gray chocolate chip, a human chocolate chip.

It began with an e-mail, November 28, 2001: "Had a thought this am. . . . Do you want to make a piece together next semester? A duet? c." Caitlin and I had been friends for a while. We were both arts faculty at Salem State College, she in dance, I in creative writing, and we both had an interest in interdisciplinary work. Earlier in the year we'd had coffee and arranged to have our students collaborate in the fall 2001 semester—her choreographers and my poets—registering the plans in our calendars.

We were going to try to make our own piece in the spring semester, then Molly, her niece, veered toward death, and Caitlin's life paused. We finally got together as the semester ended, a few months after the funeral, after the obituary I read in the *Boston Globe*.

It began back in the fall of 1999 with Eileen, my wife, saying, "When are you going to take a modern dance class?" I'd always been interested in dance, though I knew nothing about it. I was thirty-five. My basketball injuries were piling up. If not now, then when?

For the final project in that class, I had to compose a short piece. I decided to do something to one of my own writings, a paragraph of poetic prose about basketball. I spent hours leaping through my small living room, stopping, rewinding, and restarting the tape of me reading my words. Sometimes, I'd fly through the doorway into the kitchen, and my sons, eating a snack at the kitchen table, would see a flash of me and laugh.

I heard—no, felt—my words then in a way I never had before—the stresses, the caesuras, the halting rhythm of sentence fragments, my foot, landing on an accented syllable, my body taking a pass from my voice, knitting a seamless play.

It began when I nervously gave Caitlin the first poem I'd written for our collaboration, one about the photo of Molly:

Tilted
head, right arm
behind the back, fingers
curled around the left arm's inner
elbow

as if
holding her own
soft self together, or
taking her own pulse: Pah-Doom, Pah-
Doom, Pah—

Smiling
on a French road,
seventeen, a year before
her death. Tilted head angling
toward

some blue
corner of the sky,
patched with white clouds, thin
line of skin between shirt and jeans,
hips wide

as if
having given
birth already, tilted
hips, and, beside them, dangling, her
left hand

open
fingers stretching
upward, as if holding
the warm day delicately
open.

—

It began before Caitlin's e-mail, in the fall of 2001, the smoke of the World Trade Center still trailing through the country. I was driving to Cambridge once or twice a week to rehearse for a performance of the Caitlin Corbett Dance Company. I'd cross the Tobin Bridge at day's end, the buildings just beginning to flick their lights on—or off—the city spread before me in a soft orange sunset that sharpened to dark orange as I got closer and it got darker. How fragile Boston looked. I'd imagine one of the skyscrapers aflame, smoke thickening the sky, hurrying the onslaught of night.

Pay my toll, fight my way along Storrow Drive to Mass. Ave.—an opening between bikers and joggers—cross the Charles, under the colored lights in the shape of dancers that span the street, left on Pearl, right then left into the parking garage. Some days I'd arrive early and stop to get a coffee.

The piece I was in was a complex mix of movement and dancers to a mush of words, a Gary Duehr poem, "Girl and Letter." I didn't come onstage until the last segment, which contained ten dancers, arranged like bowling pins. Seven of us, the back two rows, were "nondancers," untrained folk included to add texture and, I think, noise. All ten wore belts with small tape players strapped to them, and once we were all onstage, ten different recordings of the poem would reverberate through the dance studio.

Nine of us began the dance behind a dark curtain at the back of the stage. When the lights came up, we had to have our feet far enough back so our toes weren't poking out. After each segment, the lights went down, and a new group slipped around the curtain and took its place on stage. Three high school girls occupied the row in front of me and three other thirtysomething men, and they went out just before us. The lights came on. Backstage, four men listened as the girls stomped and thumped their bodies. Their routine seemed to consist of collapsing hard, slapping the mats with their palms and heels, rising and falling, thudding incessantly. Could this noise—bodies denting air—be beauty?

I was too busy concentrating on my own moves to really comprehend the work. The movements weren't difficult, but staying in sync with the other men, and moving downstage without colliding into the other performers, made it impossible for me to follow the whole piece. After the performance, Caitlin asked me what I thought of the poem itself. "To be honest, I have no idea," I said.

It began in May 2002, when we met in her office, set up a schedule to work, gave ourselves an assignment. We were supposed to bring in both movement and a poem. Caitlin requested structure, so we decided to try cinquains, a simple five-line poem in which the lines have two, four, six, eight, and two syllables, respectively. The movement phrase was to go across the diagonal—back right to upper left—and be thirty to forty-five seconds long. The movement and the poem didn't have to be related.

I practiced in my living room, eight by twelve feet of space, starting with nothing, trying to be "artistic" but being more awkward than anything else. I added a movement with the hand, dangling it like Molly's pose in the photo—it made me almost sick doing it—it makes me almost sick thinking that I did it. The movement never made it into the final piece, never came close.

The studio, the first day, was not too hot, summer taking its time in coming. We dropped our stuff, and Caitlin started stretching. She stretched languorously, as if it were pleasure. I ran through some basketball stretches, clenching my teeth when I reached for my toes, and we talked of our students, the school, our boys (two each).

Then, we had to begin. Any awkwardness that was there was all mine. Whatever ego was there, was mine. Of course I knew then only that I didn't know what to do.

"Why don't you teach me your movement?" Caitlin said.

So I did.

Only in retrospect does one see the hubris, the absurdity, even. I, a graduate of two dance classes, believing I could make movement—make art—that was worth Caitlin's time. A few times during our sessions, my disbelief (was it guilt?) spilled over.

"Do you ever," I'd ask, "say to yourself, 'What the hell am I doing spending all this time learning these moves made up by some schmuck?'" She'd look at me as if the thought hadn't crossed her mind before, but now that I'd brought it up, she would consider it.

"What I really enjoy," she'd say, "is our interaction, our dialogue, our exchanges."

It began when Caitlin didn't know my poem was about Molly and composed movement to parts of it, thinking that I'd lost someone back when I was in high school.

It began when Caitlin, who says she never liked writing, she doesn't trust words, wrote cinquains. Four were the basis of the second half of the dance:

Breathing
with great effort
as Billie Holiday sings
to us all. We cannot sleep. We
just wait.

* * *

I see
my sister's face
as she holds her daughter
in her arms. Long limbs dangle off
the bed.

* * *

These feet
dancing on this
floor are not size 11.
But maybe we look alike?
Same eyes.

* * *

What if
Molly walked in
the room, laughed, and said,
"Today is the day that should
have been."

She wrote several others. One of the first I composed movement to was also about Molly and grief:

I can't
call my sister
without bracing myself.
She dyed her hair many colors.
Looks good.

The movement involved my body trying to sneak out of a confined space, ducking, twisting—a bit mimelike, except using legs and head, instead of hands. Caitlin watched me run it a time or two, then joined in, making movement that played off mine, speaking the words at her own pace, so that we were out of sync. Turn. Stretch. Turn. We were moving and speaking together—not at the same time, not the same movements, but together, like dancing. Soon, we tried it with other cinquains: I see I see my sister's face As she holds her daughter daughter IN HER ARMS long limbs long limbs Dangle. Off. The bed.

And so we had a way in, an idea of how the piece would work.

It began when we talked about doubt. What were we doing? "There's this fear," I said, "that it will be exploiting tragedy. You make art out of another's suffering, and then people tell you how talented you are."

"That's it," she said. "I've told my sister what we're doing. I showed her your poem. I think she would appreciate this. It's done out of love and respect, but . . ."

I quoted the poet Richard Hugo, "All great art risks sentimentality."

"I don't know about that word, 'great,'" I added.

It began when Caitlin was teaching me a movement phrase she'd created that involved some leg stretching, a bending of the torso.

I was having trouble and unconsciously was cheating, sliding and bending my leg when it should have been straight and still. Caitlin kept correcting me, and I kept noting her corrections, then doing it wrong. After the fourth time or so, I felt a twinge in my hamstring. "I might not have that flexibility," I said.

She looked doubtful. "No, it's not a question of flexibility. Here, get in this position."

I tried to imitate her, but my body wouldn't bend the way hers did.

She straightened up and appraised my contortions. "Maybe it is flexibility," she said. "Let's modify it."

It began when I noticed three words,

Skin
Cloud
Braces

at the bottom of the file with my poem—words I'd typed with my initial notes, planning to use them later. "Skin" and "Clouds" had both found their way in.

I had not liked speaking "Pah-doom, pah doom, pah," as I spun around and up out of a crouch. I'd already cut the last "pah," but even with that cut the sounds seemed a bit too comical. I heard the "oom-pah-pah" of a polka.

Why hadn't I used "braces" at first? Such an interesting word, more interesting, more specific, than "skin" or "clouds." Maybe I wasn't sure that Molly really wore braces in that picture, and I didn't want to get things wrong.

So, I took out the "pah-doom's," replaced them with those three words, each separated firmly by periods. It departed from the cinquain's syllabic pattern, but there was the same number of stressed syllables, and the pauses caused by the periods seemed like silent beats.

as if
holding her own
soft self together, or
taking her own pulse. Skin. Clouds.
Braces.

I told Caitlin that I'd changed the words a bit, and she said "OK." I guess she trusted me on the words. We ran the section a few times, and then she asked, "What was that last word?"

"Braces," I said, smiling timidly. In my mind, I saw the picture of Molly, head tilted, braces gleaming. Was this too close? Exploitative? Caitlin smiled back.

It began when Caitlin said, "It needs more texture," after she had started shouting some of the words as she spun and glided through her moves. The shouting had startled me a bit. It was immediately interesting.

Texture. I knew what she meant. I recall a poet saying that, given the choice of his writing being flashy and shallow or boring and deep, he'd prefer the latter. I wouldn't want to settle for either. Art must excite, must constantly surprise. We'd composed several fragments—movement to individual cinquains—and were planning to stitch them together eventually. Our fragments were good first steps, but they all had the same feel. We'd both be moving, and, usually, we'd both be saying words. There was variation—sometimes one would speak, sometimes we'd speak in unison, sometimes we'd speak deliberately out of sync, but we spoke the words plainly, flatly, and our movements, while containing some compelling gestures, all seemed to be at the same moderate speed. It needed texture.

The texture we found was not with our voices but in our movements. During one practice Caitlin said, "Why don't you fall into me?" The great unspoken. Touching. So simple, so . . . We ran through our movements, and I fell toward her left shoulder. We were pressing against each other. Now what? She suggested we try to shift our weight—"Hook your arm around me. I'll hold you like this." Her hand holding my waist. My arm angled across her back, hand clutching her hip. "Not so hard," she said. Not so hard. We kept moving—separating. I clutched her wrist and helped her fall gently to the dance floor, then spun away, saying the poem's next words: "as if."

And so it became acceptable to touch, and soon we had choreographed an interlude with no words that we placed between my cinquains and hers. In the section we collided with each other, hauled each other off the floor, gave each other small pushes. When we would finish dancing the section, and Caitlin spun and began her words that opened the second half of the dance, she was winded, and spoke with great effort.

It began with silences, moments too heavy for words. We'd be talking about the piece, how to arrange some words and movement, and grief would step into the studio, seethe in a corner. Should we walk back together or apart at the end? I tried to explain how together felt like a more positive ending, something in unison, a more hopeful sense than us being disconnected, moving in opposition to each other. But then I shut up. The notions, the creation, had to wait, had to recognize the presence of fact, of death, the truth of loss. Gone. No art. No talk. Let it be. . . . And I'd glance at the mirrored walls, see myself looking sad and troubled, and sweaty, and definitely alive. The glowing wood floor felt just strong enough to hold us up.

It began a few days before the performance, when Caitlin looked over her shoulder at me and said, "We might not be done with this."

It began when, during one rehearsal, near the end, Caitlin said, "I think it's so interesting that you say 'Braces.' Molly never wore braces."

"She didn't?" I was shocked, and then troubled. "Now I've got to change that."

"I thought it was OK. I thought you were referring to the other kind of braces—support—and she had so many things inside of her by the end, shunts and . . . things to help hold her together."

Now what?

I kept "braces," but maybe, if we do it again, I'll say "shunts," even though they don't appear in the photo either.

It began when we had drafted the whole dance and realized, as we looked back over the video of our early movement, that we had forgotten about the piece we'd composed to "*I can't . . .*"—the one in which we first found a way to move and speak together.

We watched it on video. "I like it," we both said, shrugging. We relearned it, added it in the middle of the piece, the section without speech. No. We liked the spell of silence, and, we realized, the words should go later in the piece, toward the end of Caitlin's sequence of cinquains—after the poems in which Molly was still alive, before the last two.

It seemed like a good fit at that moment on stage. We were already clustered in the corner, positioned to move into it easily and naturally. There would be no struggle with transitions.

It just didn't work, though. The section that preceded it consisted of us moving about in a limited space—the lower left corner of the stage, and the "*I can't*" section didn't travel much, either. The piece seemed cramped, bogged down, and we were repeating the word "sister," which sounded clunky.

"It feels good to run out of here," Caitlin said. Neither of us liked spending so much time in one place.

We took it out. Its echo is in two words, "sister" and "braces."

It began when Caitlin said, "I cried in front of my class today. Have you ever done that?"

I haven't. Not yet. Not quite.

The class had been sitting in a circle in the dance studio, discussing possible titles for the piece Caitlin had made for them to perform. The piece was also about Molly—Caitlin said it was "very sweet, even sappy." The music was Molly's favorite song, "Somewhere Over the Rainbow." Caitlin had told the class the whole story a few weeks previously, and in the last class, had asked them to offer possible titles. They were going around the circle, sharing possibilities, and one dancer said, "Molly's Rainbow."

"That's it," everyone said. And Caitlin burst into tears. "It came so suddenly," she said.

It began when I accepted that I never knew Molly, would never know her. I knew her through Caitlin's grief and her beauty. I knew her through Caitlin's movement, through Caitlin's art. I knew her through Caitlin.

It began the Sunday morning, a day before the performance. Caitlin had brought juices and scones for the dozen students who'd come to help set up before the dress rehearsal. A student and I began unrolling the marley, the strips of dance floor that needed to be put down in the gym. We knelt and pushed. "Actually," said Caitlin, "it works better if you kick it."

"How are you feeling about it?" I asked her a few minutes later as we unlocked the storage room door and stepped past boxes of tennis rackets and gymnastics mats to get to the sound system. She stopped and thought—was she trying to be honest, or diplomatic?—"I wish I danced it better," she said.

We might not be done with this.

It began in my living room, rug pushed back. I, barefooted.

It began when we tilted our heads, lifted our right legs and said, "Tilted."

It began with Eileen and Aidan, my seven-year-old son, watching in the front row.

It began.

LIVING THE OUTFIELD

The outfield stretches from the flat, dried brown grass of Fairview Park in Normal, Illinois, to the thick green behind the high school tennis courts in New Milford, Connecticut, to Furlong Field in Salem, Massachusetts, booby-trapped with gooseshit, hemmed in on three sides by an auto junkyard, a playground, and a street, but, on its fourth side—is that fair territory?—sloping down into the mouth of the North River as it drifts into the Atlantic.

Its boundaries are inexact, and infinite—a state of mind.

It's a dumping ground for the weak-armed, the unskilled, the left-handed; its grasses are littered with failures. Even Whitman, the supreme outfielder (unshaven, musing, great range) would be perplexed by grass so full of misjudgments.

The outfield is tainted with mercury and lead paint; it's an old Indian burial ground. Ambiguous weeds make love to lost strands of grass in the shadow of an imaginary scoreboard. The brown patches where the outfielders usually stand weep like bullet holes. A hollow anonymous voice slurs facts that pile in soggy heaps down the left-field line.

There are no fathers and sons in the outfield. There is, somehow, not enough room. Beyond the foul lines, there have been sightings of gnarled gods with curious, knobby protrusions and unpronounceable names—the sentimental call them angels.

The low line drive skims the infield and bounds toward you, a little to your right. Nobody on, one out. You need simply to stop the ball. The throw, which needn't be rushed, will go to the shortstop, who is lining himself up with second base. The ball is still moving fast, but it's on the ground. Plant one knee in the grass, the other bent, leg opening out. The glove touches the ground, throwing hand beside it, fingers splayed. Watch the ball into the glove, closing your hand over it, getting hold of it as you push yourself up, angling your body in line with second. The arm drops and rises behind you, your glove points to your target, then falls as you shift your weight and release. Whooshhhhhh—snap! into the shortstop's mitt. The shortstop turns and jogs the few steps to the infield dirt, watching the runner retreat to first, then flips to the pitcher. Single.

Mostly, the outfielder runs to back up, to collect a poor throw, or a surprising bounce, to limit others' mistakes, to assure everyone that things are not *that* bad. Hustle behind third base. Be ready for the pickoff to second, the overthrow from third to first. Mostly—and ideally—these efforts are unrewarded. The play is made, the outfielder jogs back to his post, glove unused, breath easing to normal, perhaps hollering, "Good play" or, "Way to do it," as he folds into position, knees bent, hand and glove on them. Settled, he spits, as if saying, *That's done.*

If things go perfectly, the pitcher never lets the ball leave the infield. Logically, the outfielder's ideal game is one in which he does nothing. There he is, scuffing the grass with his cleat, spitting sunflower seeds, offering some bland encouragement that the pitcher may not even hear. There he is, lying down and staring up at the empty, endless sky, the greatest outfield, uncoverable. He plucks a blade of grass and pins it between his teeth. A plane leaves a contrail that connects one cloud to another. It is just cool enough that when a breeze passes, goose bumps appear on his arms.

The outfield, even center field, is not for strivers, those cursed with ambition or pride. Lear ends up in the outfield, raging in a storm (why didn't they call the game?), but he never imagined he would be out there, rain spilling from his cap's brim.

The outfield is democratic. Anyone can play it, and, let's admit, any number can play it. Twelve players on your team? Have six outfielders.

This country, drifting toward empire, more proud than democratic, has little interest in the outfield. In the major leagues, the fences keep getting closer and closer. The possibilities, the players, must be hemmed in.

Watch an infielder groom his position, bending every now and then to pick up a small rock and toss it beyond the baseline, out of play. Such fastidiousness! Obsessive compulsive, clean shaven or finely mustachioed, they are too tidy. *Are my pants too loose? My socks the right height? Is my cap precisely centered and angled off the forehead?*

What can an outfielder do? The task is Sisyphean. One can't tidy the universe. Pick up a rock or dirt clod and move it . . . where? And what about the other rocks, pebbles, twigs? The logs and memories and boulders? A ball could go anywhere. One must resign oneself to fate—the ball will collide with what it chooses. The world will go where it goes. You are not central to its outcome. The bombs will fall, and you can do little to stop them. Back up! Always back up! Or, if the situation calls for it, run like hell, holding your glove ahead of you like an offering, or a prayer.

In a time of war, the outfield may be your only chance.

Turn to the right fielder, the young guy who is supposed to be good, the one who aches for your position, and yell "Kevin!" When he turns, open and close your mouth as if you are talking, but, rather than say words, just let out occasional syllables—"Ah-Bo-Ace-Ta-Ta-Jedda." Smile as if you've said something clever. Watch him smile, nod, and offer a weak laugh. What pleasure to be goofy! He thinks you're annoying, or nuts. He's certain that you're not as good as he is (he belongs in the infield). Lift your cap off your head, rub your long hair off your brow with your arm, then get ready for the pitch.

In the outfield, I smoked pot. I cracked stupid jokes about sex that I only half understood. I rode in cars, their tires cutting the turf, making ridges in the moonlight. I stood in line, waiting for my turn, for the coach to hit me ten fly balls in a row until my arm burned from all those throws back in, until my lungs burned from all that running.

In the outfield, I composed the great song of the spheres that I will never sing aloud, that I have half forgotten now, as I enter middle age.

In the outfield, worms eased between the nubs of my cleats, trying to write their damp hieroglyphics on my soles.

Yes, we were naked in the outfield, and I can hardly remember her now, but it was good.

In the silences of center field, I etched haikus on the back of my glove:

> I was of three minds,
> like an outfield, in which there
> are three outfielders.

From a distance, the outfielder stands, small and thin, a young boy's erect penis, so insignificant on the huge body of the field. Something passing over him that is vague, unknown, presexual, keeps him from dropping limp on the grass. The breeze? The clouds? Whitman's trembling hand? The pitch?

The outfielder's pleasure is simple, unencumbered by guilt or desire: See ball. Chase ball. Get ball. Throw ball. Oh, joy!

The outfielder does not wear a protective cup. He does not speak of fences.

You have taken a turn on the pitcher's mound, and spent a little glamour time at shortstop, but you have always been an outfielder. When you were nine, playing in a league of nine- and ten-year-olds, you were the worst hitter on a first-place team. You spent that season excited and terrified, standing on the fringes of the outfield. Kids rarely hit the ball farther than the edge of the infield dirt. One game, the main slugger on the other team, a kid named Todd Whitehouse, hit a monstrous fly ball out toward you. You watched it. You stepped toward it. You caught it. And you were baptized an outfielder, teammates slapping your back and hollering. Since then, you've believed you can catch any ball that you can reach, and most that you can't.

A secret: true outfielders abhor hitting. To be the spectacle—how distressingly public. And, it's so violent, brutal. Batting is something the outfielder accepts, penance for the joy of hunting fly balls, a kind of tax.

It is hardly worth running hard if you don't get to dive, stretching parallel to the ground and falling into it at the end. The batter begins to swing, and before he even hits the ball, you're taking a step left or right, depending on the pitch location and the speed of the swing. The ball moves up and out, and you are moving too, your body calculating geometry on the run—the best angle, the quickest route, exactly where the little fucker is going. You're running so hard you forget you're running, and you lose all the awkward hitches that make you slower than you should be. Whisk, whisk, across the grass, whisk, whisk. And the ball comes down, and your body calculates again—is a dive necessary? If so, how? What angle? Off which leg? Now! The arm stretches. . . . Snap! Thud! It's in the glove. You're on the ground. You hop up and hurl the ball back to the infield, back from whence it came, and feel your chest rise and fall, rise and fall. When you lie down tonight, your side will be tender, and you will be unable to sleep, your chest still rising and falling, your mind chasing that ball down in the great dark field of night.

SPIN MOVES

I have been doing research. Ninety-degree Indiana summer, humidity like a shirt, sun burning my shoulders, my bare chest and back. I limp on my bruised heel, grimace when decorum requires, cry out "Yo," "Swing it," "Let it go," "My man," "Sweet," "Who's got him?" "Nice cut."

Between games we collapse in the shade of a nearby tree, taking turns standing and drinking from the water jug, rattling with ice, that Clay has looped over a branch. Clay lets the water fall onto his forehead and down his face, red as meat, then turns his head to the ground, the stream now on his neck, drops running down his bronze back. He removes his finger; the water stops; and he stands and shakes his head, sighs with relief, or pleasure.

Roy, his long bushy hair tied in a ponytail today to lessen the heat, lies on his back in the grass, arms out, eyes closed. His pale heavy body rises and falls. His game, a combination of sweet shooting and an occasional smooth, if slow, drive, prompted some black guys he played once to call him "Larry Legend." When his shot's falling, we call him Larry.

Roy's two kids run over, ask if they can go home. Dirty, sweaty, and pudgy, they seem wiser than the rest of us: "It's too hot," they whine.

"Sit in the shade," Roy says, "Don't run around if you're hot. Just one more game." He stands up, reaches into the crook of the tree, and removes a cigarette from his pack. He lights it and sits, elbows on knees. Despite his weight, his smoking, and the heat, he'll get up and play the next game the way he always plays. He'll drain his shots and stand in the lane on defense, catching his breath, giving his man the eight-foot chip shot.

Fred is back on the court, taking shots, waiting for the next game. He's talking to Mary and me about his upcoming vacation to Wisconsin. Elena sulks around the court's borders, angry at her shoulder's failures, its pain. Mark is discussing the last game with whoever will listen.

It is a local park, Bryan Park. Children climb on the nearby playground, zip down the slide, hopping on the bits of tire that have been put down to prevent injury, a Bloomington recycling project. All too often, some of these bite-sized nuggets sprinkle the court. Sometimes, we sweep them off with our feet, swishing arcs on the asphalt, herding them out of bounds. Sometimes we play regardless, accepting the occasional off bounce.

The two courts are painted green, the lanes red, the lines white. There is no three-point line, which is good—no reason to encourage low-percentage gunning in pickup games. A few summers ago, the city replaced the plain iron rims with doubly enforced rings—two inches of metal before the net begins. These rims are solid and, coupled with the grill-metal backboards, remarkably unfriendly.

By bike, it is a two-minute ride from my house to the park. I travel down Fess Ave., under its shady oaks and maples, the street lightly speckled with sun. Cross Second, Park, First, Maxwell. The last twenty seconds are the most exhilarating: when the street dead-ends and I launch my bike onto the slightly sloping grass of the park's northern limits. I can't see the court yet, but I can see the backboards, and the occasional rise and fall of a ball, like a ping-pong ball in a lottery canister. The pool, with its long corkscrew slide, shimmers in the distant left, and straight ahead, beyond the courts and over the stream, stretch the softball diamonds, the nearest usually filled with a coed group—shorts and T-shirts.

The courts themselves appear only after I have cruised by the small wood and metal exercise area, shuddered across the gravel jogging path, and drawn even with the empty picnic pavilion on my right. From here, a sharp descent sends me speeding to the base of the nearest court, where I lock my bike to a sapling.

The moment before the final rush: that's when I survey the morning. I make a quick note of the people—who, how many. I figure, based on the time, if we will get enough for full court. A wince for each mediocre player. If it rained the night before, I scan for puddles.

Saturday mornings, ten o'clock. Off and on, for eight years, a group of men and women plays basketball. The ever-changing roster: John, Karl, Jim, Jon, Rick, Bill F., Roy, Joe, Ryan, Mark, Fred, Steve, Elena, Mary, Karen, Rich, Clay, Jay, David, Jeff, Kosmo, David C., Bill L., Michael, Ethan, Adam, Kit, K.C., Linda, Emily, Andrew, Rob, Rachel, James, Big Dave, Josh.

Few of them play anymore. If they're lucky, they get six players. Some have moved, some work weekends, some have injuries or families that they don't want to risk aggravating. Neither I, nor my two closest friends from the group, Mary and Mark, are playing much ball right now. I'm in Salem, recovering from reconstructive surgery on my knee. Mark's still in Bloomington, but he's only played once in the last six months. He's got a bad back that keeps him up some nights. Mary's moved to Washington, D.C., and her cancer, which had been in remission, has metastasized. It's in her lungs.

More than a friend, Mary has been a moral force in my life, one of the few people I imagine reading my words when I write. Her presence keeps me honest—as honest as I can be anyway. Before Dave, her husband, moved to Indiana, Mary lived in a house with four other English graduate students. One night the house threw a party. In the kitchen a group of us drank beers and leaned against the counters. Someone proposed that we should forsake literature and teach students to interpret television and film, since those were the most influential media in their lives. I agreed.

Mary almost squealed in disappointment.

"Oh J.D., you can't believe that."

I can't. I don't. At the time, I offered a half-hearted defense, but I knew that she was right, that I had been posing.

Once, my wife, Eileen, and I were discussing the miracle of circumstance that had brought us together. Why us? We tested out and rejected friends that we had known as potential alternative mates. "I don't think I could live with anyone else," I said. A pause.

"Mary," we both said.

Mary and Dave lived a few blocks away. Mark and his wife, Colleen, lived in an apartment on Second Street, just around the corner from the house Eileen and I rented on Fess. Through the rosebuds screening our porch, we could see their brick building, which Eileen always thought looked like a convent. We loved our house. Fairly low rent, and much bigger than we needed: two bedrooms, a huge kitchen, a large open living-dining area, and the porch where we'd watch students walking to or from class, or listen to the guitar player across the street, strumming and singing Neil Young songs. Occasionally, a few ballplayers would hang out on the porch after basketball, drinking water, soda, beer, the shadows of leaves flitting on us, someone rocking on the porch swing. When we moved to Madison, Wisconsin, in 1994, we arranged for Mary and Dave to move into the house. We didn't want to see it go to a stranger.

Before we moved we'd get together, three couples. We'd watch bad sci-fi horror movies, usually about giant radioactive insects, or we'd watch basketball: Indiana University, or the NCAA tournament. Among the topics of conversation was our weekly game. Mary, Mark, and I would analyze the players' skills and personalities, and our bored spouses would nod and smile.

The six of us had, and still have, our own NCAA tournament pool, in which the person who finishes last bakes cookies for the winner. The cookie pool. In the spring of 1995, the year after we had moved, Mary lost the cookie pool to me a week or so after she first found out she had breast cancer. "Obviously, there's no justice in this world," she'd said over the phone. She had called to congratulate me and to tell us that because of the cancer, she and Dave and Mark and Colleen wouldn't be making the seven-hour drive to Madison to watch the NCAA finals with us.

A few weeks later, her raisin oatmeal cookies arrived in a taped box, crumbled but still tasty.

In my sophomore year of high school, I cried after an intramural basketball game. I sobbed uncontrollably in my bedroom, and I finally had to go to my parents to let them calm me down. For five minutes, I couldn't stop.

It was after one of the two games I remember from that year, but I can't recall which one. One game, I'd played hard and well, but our team lost by one point on a last-second shot by a kid who later would become a casual friend and companion in vandalism. Ron had dribbled to the corner, almost out of bounds, and I had followed determinedly. In desperation, he jumped and heaved the ball toward the basket. "No way," I said to myself, turning. The ball, off target, skimmed the backboard and, kindly redirected, slanted through the net.

If I didn't cry after that game, then it was after a game our team won in overtime. The referee, an upperclassman, a star fullback, counted out the final seconds—five, four, three. I was trailing a teammate who had dribbled frantically upcourt, then picked up the ball and been swarmed by two defenders.

"Greg," I called.

He turned and grimaced. He really wanted to shoot, but, cornered, he flipped the ball back. On the wing, twenty feet out, I went up. Focused on the basket, I released, then tilted my head to watch the ball's arc against the off-white supports crisscrossing the ceiling. Two points. Game.

Greg was the first one to reach me, grabbing me around the waist and hoisting me in the air. The rest of the team crowded around, slapping my hands or pounding my back.

It was over in seconds. And then, each of us walked out of the gym, separately or in groups of two or three. As I walked past the upperclassman referee, I overheard him say to the other ref, "Lucky little shit," in a voice loaded with scorn, even contempt.

I slunk out alone, started the two-block trudge home through the snowy dark. I stepped over the flattened fence in back of the parking lot and followed the backyard paths until I reached my street, Caldwell Drive. There are no sidewalks, and I walked down the middle of the street, the thin coat of snow pressed into the grooves of my leather Nike high-tops.

Two years later, I cried again. This time, too, it was in front of my parents. I had been in a car with some friends—including Ron—and they (not me, not me!) had hurled empty beer bottles at two hitchhikers, then turned back, and though one of the hitchhikers was curled in the gravel, obviously hurt, they threw more bottles. Quietly, I asked to be taken home. That night, late, I stumbled into my parents' bedroom and confessed.

This was during the same winter I finally made the basketball team: a senior who rarely played, who never scored a point.

—

Before he returned to Bloomington in 1993, Mark, who has just turned forty, spent two years in Machias, way Down East in Maine, picking blueberries most of the summer and refusing to turn on the heat in the winter. He and Colleen, a Legal Services lawyer, spent those winters huddled under blankets, watching ESPN and reading, able to see their own breath over the bed. He didn't play ball all that time, just a handball game every few days. Giving up ball was a huge concession, but Mark might have been willing to make it for Machias's isolation. If Colleen's job hadn't ended, it's possible they would have never left.

It is not simply important, but essential, that Colleen work. This is because it is also essential, apparently, that Mark work for less than six dollars an hour. Despite allegedly having a college degree from a tiny school named after a saint in western Pennsylvania, Mark has never done anything but manual labor. He's never had a driver's license or a credit card. Now he works part-time in the receiving department of bookstores until, we like to joke, his aura drives the business into bankruptcy. In many ways, he's a hard, dedicated worker. His bosses are strangely drawn to him, and he's been offered full-time positions (managerial posts) at all these places, but he's turned them down, earnestly, with such lines as "The truth is, this job is boring. I can give you twenty good hours, twenty-five tops." He is unable to interact with customers. If he happens to be "on the floor" and a customer asks him a question, he feigns deafness, drifting behind a bookshelf.

I believe Mark's explanations for rejecting higher-paying full-time positions. He loathes the thought of having authority. But there is another reason why he stays part-time: he needs to play basketball. He plays in the Saturday morning game, and with a group of locals, faculty, and staff at noon three days a week at Indiana University.

Mark befriended a man, Randy, at the park, whom he invited to the Saturday morning game. Randy tended to foul people hard, accidentally, but he was a good guy. After a month or two, it came out that Randy was a biologist in Bloomington for a year on a prestigious fellowship, a genius award of a hundred thousand dollars. Randy offered Mark ten thousand dollars. Don't worry about working, Randy told him, "you should be playing basketball." Mark nobly turned him down.

The friendships developed in basketball, while often limited to a pick-and-roll on court and small talk while waiting for the next game, are enduring. I meet someone I played with for a summer years ago, and we shake hands, ask each other, "How's it going?" This is how Mark and I first became friends. I'd played with him a few times the summer before he went to Maine, and when, two years later, he reappeared at the court one Saturday morning, I smiled. We shook hands. "I remember you. You're a good passer," I said. Within weeks, I had invited him and Colleen over to dinner with Mary and Dave. We had homemade pesto pizza and shared stories, including how Mark and Colleen met at a wedding. "I'm an anarchist," Mark had said, "Wanna dance?"

"How do you just go down and start playing with people you don't know?" Eileen asks.

Whenever I move to a new place, I seek out the courts, hope to get into a regular game. It's not just the run but the socialization. I don't mean locker-room talk after the games—there's very little of that unless you're stuck playing with teenagers. I don't even desire the casual conversations between or after games, the beers at the bar, although those are always nice. It's the human contact on the court, eyes linking with the other player, saying, "Backdoor." Moving to set a pick, hand discreetly gesturing to your teammate, "Come this way." The sweet signals of approval: the nod of the head or the quick slap of hands after a basket. These moments are unusual, even rare. One needs to be playing with someone who understands the game, who appreciates it.

I became friends with Mark because of his sweet no-look passes, his great give-and-go.

Mark is one of the few people I can talk with openly about basketball. Sometimes, we simply talk moves. Standing on the court, ball cocked at the shoulder, he analyzes my crossover dribble. I tell him how I try to play his turnaround fadeaway, and we go through both moves, slowly, breaking them down, discussing the strengths and vulnerabilities of each.

Sometimes, there's more. Walking back from the gym, we talk of how making a certain move or shot triggered vivid images of similar moments when we were young. The shots don't need to be spectacular; in fact, perhaps it is the opposite of the spectacular that recalls the past: the repetition of a well-known move, done to perfection so that it is the ideal, the archetype, the ur-move, a move in which the body seems outside of time. The crossover dribble and the push off the legs, the straightening of the body, the arm rising, the wrist flicking: the whole motion more of a body essence than a body moving through time and space. And that same essence, on the indoor court of a private high school against some guys you thought were old then, when you were nineteen. That same move outdoors, at the courts adjacent to the town's softball fields—Young's Field—when you were sixteen and just learning the game and it felt right for once, finally! And making that move this day brings back all those days down at Young's Field, not in a rush of games, or even the memory of a particular move, but the sense of those days past. The crisp autumn air, the man searching the grove of trees near the court for cans, the worn brown ball, hide too soft, like fine fur, the sweatshirt, dirty at its fringes, always falling down your arms and rubbing against your wrists.

Once, Mark spotted *Foul: The Connie Hawkins Story* on my coffee table. "That's a great book," he said. He was fifteen when the book had first been published, and he and a friend, Jay, split the cost of a hardback. They took it to the courts in Paterson, New Jersey, and read aloud to each other between games. Read a chapter, play ball—a strange basketball foreplay. I understood. When I would watch an NBA playoff game, I'd be changing into my shorts as half-time approached to go out and shoot in the driveway.

Another Mark story: One day when Mark and Jay were in fifth grade, they got out of their Catholic school and realized that winter had withdrawn enough so that they could shoot hoops outside. They cast off their school sweaters and raced to the courts in the T-shirts they always wore underneath, so that they would be prepared for this moment. And they played, in T-shirts and brown pants. Mark didn't say, but I bet they played until it got too dark to see the ball, and then, maybe, they played a little longer.

A while back, in the town where I lived, a twenty-three-year-old man pushed a round object, about ten inches in diameter, away from him, angling it toward the wooden floor. The object bounced and rose into the hands of another man who was running quickly and who kept running, bouncing the ball to himself. A few moments later, the twenty-three-year-old was grabbed by an older man with a tight clump of gray hair and a paunch covered with an ill-fitting red sweater. The older man flung the twenty-three-year-old down into a chair, then knelt and, his face within six inches of the other man's face, began yelling. After a few moments, he stood up and swung his foot at the younger man, striking him in the leg.

This is part of basketball in Indiana. This is what former Indiana University coach, Bob Knight, did to his son for making a bad pass.

My basketball education did not start in the small, upstairs gym at New Milford High School where I fell in love with the game—where I played after school, taking off my button-down shirt and playing bare-chested in long pants and a pair of Nikes. It didn't even start my senior year when I made the team and rode the bench. I was so little a part of that team that I don't believe I ever learned the offense or defense. Nor in my four years at Columbia, in any of the games I played in the school's gym (including the intramural championship) or in Riverside Park (where I once threw an alley-oop to an eighth-grader who could, and did, dunk it). It started the year before I moved out to Indiana at Warren, a small high school in northwestern Connecticut where I was the assistant coach for one year, coaching under Brian McCarthy, a Bobby Knight disciple.

"I could play for him," McCarthy told me once. He was referring not to his physical abilities—he couldn't have played for Indiana; he wasn't as good as me—but to his mental fortitude.

"I'm not sure I'd want to," I said.

I learned a lot that year. Coaching made me realize what I never had realized as a player or as a fan: the importance athletics can play in self-development. As the season progressed, I realized that I wanted to make my players feel happy, confident, even loved.

A win was good, too.

Warren's colors were red and white, like Indiana's, and McCarthy fashioned himself a high school version of Knight. One practice consisted of the team going into an empty classroom and watching an hour-long video of Knight teaching basketball. Another time, about a third of the way through the season, McCarthy flung his clipboard across the gym in a Knight-like tirade, frustrated by the team's mediocre performance in a drill. I was standing on the sideline when he blew the whistle, and the clipboard zipped two feet behind me at ankle level before skimming and sliding under the folded wooden bleachers. The pencil rolled harmlessly to a stop, the only noise in the gym.

"Get out of here!" he screamed. "If you're not going to make the effort, then just get out!"

By this point in the season, the players were thoroughly terrified of McCarthy, but they were puzzled now. They stood, hands at their sides, waiting for an explanation. Was this a water break?

McCarthy realized his miscalculation immediately. These kids, generally wealthy and not devoted to basketball, these kids who went skiing every chance they could, just didn't understand.

"Why practice when you aren't going to make the effort? Practice is over. Get the hell out of here!"

Still, the players weren't quite clear. The logic didn't follow. We screwed up, so we get to go home early? A few of them began shuffling their feet. One of the captains, thinking that McCarthy just wanted renewed commitment, barked, "C'mon guys!"

"Get out. Hit the showers. Practice is over." If McCarthy had another clipboard, he would have thrown it, too. His tactic was bombing. The players slipped out. A few shrugged discreetly.

As the players left, McCarthy called me to him. I jogged over. "J.D., go in there and tell them they've got to get their act together. Let them know I'm angry." I almost groaned aloud, knowing this pathetic good-cop–bad-cop routine would flop. (Sure enough, when I went into the locker room, they were all horsing around, snapping towels at each other and laughing. I mumbled a few words, told them to take it easy, and walked out.)

"ok," I said. Assistant coaches are notorious yes-men.

"Thanks. See you tomorrow." He turned to the team manager, "Ken, could you bring the clipboard to my office?"

We were a bad team (we finished 4-16) playing a mediocre team: Goshen, a regional high school in a community of less than ten thousand. We were a class S school, as were most of the teams in the league. S stands for small, but in our case S could have stood for short: our center was 6 foot, our starting forwards 6'1" and 5'11". In Goshen's case, S could have stood for slow. All of their players had the same pear-shaped build. Too much tv. It was an even match.

We were homered, no doubt. This is the nature of basketball, especially high school basketball in the Berkshire League. Still, this was a mildly remarkable case.

The gym was small, with a few bleachers on either side of the court. The walls, covered with protective padding, stood a few feet behind each baseline. On one end was the gym's entrance, where booster-club mothers sold tickets at a table, and a man in a dark blue sweater and white shirt—blue and white were Goshen's colors—promptly collected them, dropped them in a box, and stamped the person's hand. Right next to him, leaning against the padding, was a red-faced policeman with a puffy mustache. His dark blue suit was almost black, and he wore his badge over his left breast.

The teams sat on the bottom row of the bleachers. There was a gap in the bleachers at half-court, and seated there, at a school desk, was the announcer. He had a microphone, and taped to the desk were two sheets of paper with the two teams' rosters. He announced a player's name when a player scored or entered the game, and players waiting to enter the game would kneel at the desk. Behind and above this man, at an elevated counter attached to the bleachers, sat the official scorers, a man and two women, probably teachers or parents, responsible for the clock and the scoreboard.

With one minute left in the game, a foul was called on our best player, our six-foot senior center, Peter Benton. Even today, I see him waiting, feet planted, hands stretching straight toward the ceiling, as the Goshen player lifts his knee and tries to go through him.

Sure, it looked like a bad call to me, but it was the kind you expect, the kind that are in our favor when we play at home. This was Peter's fifth foul, so we had to replace him, and McCarthy chose to send in the backup freshman guard, Jerry Valente. Sitting on the bench, I checked the scoreboard—0:57—and then watched McCarthy, his arm around Jerry's shoulders, give instructions. Actually, he was probably just reminding him whom to guard, then babbling something about getting tough. Coaches generally take advantage of the full thirty seconds allotted to select a replacement to do some extra coaching, and McCarthy always wanted to be a real coach.

Finally he slapped Jerry on the ass. "Go check in." By this time, the whole gym was tuned to the exchange, waiting for the game to resume. The referee stood at the foul line, ball sitting on one palm, his other arm raised, whistle propped between his lips. All the other players were lined up along the lane, heads turned.

Checking into a game is the most informal formality in basketball. Usually the official scorers notice when a coach is going to send someone in, and often, as a courtesy, they will sound the horn for a substitution even before the player reaches the scoring table so that he can go in before the refs resume play.

Jerry took two steps and tapped the announcer's desk. "I'm going in."

He jogged toward the foul line to take his spot. He hadn't taken five or six steps when a cry came from the official scorers at their table in the stands.

"You have to check in. You have to check in."

Jerry stopped, turned, and had just begun to jog back when a whistle blew, and the ref at the foul line came running over, dropping the ball, signaling T with his hands.

"Violation. Technical foul."

Somehow, McCarthy did not explode. I still cannot figure out why. He had spent the entire game in his usual frenzied state, screaming at his players and at the referees. The first game of the season, he leapt from the bench just after the opening tip and began to berate the refs so harshly that people simply stared and forgot to watch the game. The other coach kept looking over, aghast. I feared he had gone crazy. When I realized he hadn't, I felt ashamed to be associated with him, to be on the same bench.

Perhaps at this moment McCarthy wanted to win so desperately that he did not want to risk another technical. Perhaps he was realizing then what I have come to realize only now, writing this: the refs hated him, and this was their revenge for his obnoxiousness. Whatever the reason, he just stood there, his face crimson, his neck muscles visible, taut.

"That's a horrible call, Jack. A horrible call. Let the players decide the game," he said. He was angry and loud, but he wasn't screaming.

"Two shots," the ref said, ignoring him. The crowd was just beginning to understand what had happened, and, though stunned by the remarkably improbable call, it began to clap, slowly but determinedly. Even Goshen's most dedicated fans seemed a bit embarrassed about the ref's audacity. Heads shook, eyes rolled, smiles were exchanged.

We lost by three. The fans cheered, then stood, gathering their coats, their scarves and hats. The players lined up to shake hands. Slap.

"Good game." Slap. "Good game." Suddenly, Alan Heath, our power forward, and one of Goshen's players were swinging at each other. A few others paired off. Shouts, swears, screams from the crowd as it swarmed the court.

I was the first one to Alan, pulling him away. McCarthy saw the melee and turned to Goshen's coach: "See, this is what you get." The coach, moving to break up the fight himself, looked at McCarthy and yelled something back. Fortunately, the crowd didn't begin swinging—they were just parents trying to reestablish sanity—though a few barked threats.

"To the locker room," someone said, and I helped herd the team there, circling my arms around them. I ended up chest to chest with Saul Davis, our cocaptain, a 5'7" Mormon. Saul was backing up slowly, looking over my shoulder at Goshen's players, his face tight with panic and hate, teeth bared.

Then, a shot of whiskey breath over my shoulder, and an arm reaching past me, pushing Saul in the chest. The voice: "We got a place for punks like you." I turned and saw a bulbous red nose, a badge pinned against navy blue. This was the man responsible for keeping order. He had a gun in his holster.

"Move it," I said to Saul. He did.

In the locker room under the gym, the players were hyper. "God damn it," one roared, then pounded his fist into a locker. McCarthy came down soon. "Shower up," he said. He made eye contact with our two captains. "Peter, Saul. I want to talk to you after you're dressed."

McCarthy and I slipped into a side room, a shower room for coaches. We both were sweating through our suits. He grinned.

"Crazy," he said.

Still stunned, I shook my head. "How're we going to get out of here?"

"We've got a police escort."

I didn't mention the drunken cop.

McCarthy gave another grin, then sheepishly tried to hide it. He hardened his face. "What should we tell them?"

That was easy. "Look," I said, "you've got to make clear that this can never, ever, ever happen again. Someone could have been killed."

"Right. Absolutely."

One of the school officials came into the locker room and explained to us the procedure for getting out. Single file to the bus. Don't say anything. Don't turn our heads. The police would follow us to the town line.

Soon Peter and Saul stood before us in the tiny room, their wet hair flat on their heads, dress shirts damp from the steam. The rest of the team milled among the lockers, shoes sliding and clacking on the tiles. A burst of laughter. McCarthy poked his head out. "Hey!" he shouted, glaring. Silence.

McCarthy turned back to Peter and Saul. He clutched his clipboard in his right hand, jabbing it for emphasis.

"Guys, I really admire the intensity . . ."

I wanted to stop him right there. I should've, but I didn't. Peter and Saul kept breathing deeply as they nodded through the speech, their adrenaline draining. Once when McCarthy paused, I threw in "never, ever again," but they ignored me. They had gotten the message. They had pleased their coach. He admired their intensity.

When McCarthy finished, he put his clipboard under his arm and clapped his hands twice, the same gesture he used to encourage the team during games. We went into the room where the other players were waiting, and McCarthy told them how we were to board the bus. The players looked scared. It was the same look they had whenever they took a bad shot or threw a ball away, anticipating McCarthy's wrath.

"ok," he said, "follow me."

He was Train.

At twenty-six, Travis Raines was arrested, charged with possession of marijuana and cocaine with intent to sell. Even though I lived eight hundred miles from New Milford, Connecticut, where the arrest occurred, I felt the tremor the news sent through the town. Train arrested. Despite the newspaper label, it didn't quite seem a "tragedy." Rather, it served as a confirmation of the fleeting nature of high school athletic fame, a fact most of us who had known Train, or had seen him play, were just beginning to recognize. Train's arrest though, did not signal how the mighty had fallen, but reminded us how small all of our lives were. We may not have been arrested, but we were still treading water, borrowing money from our parents or working a job we hated to pay for the children we hadn't been planning on so soon. If Train was arrested, well, at least he was getting his name in the paper. Just like the old days.

Possession of marijuana and cocaine with intent to sell. How many times had we smoked weed together? Four, maybe five. After a basketball game once, five of us players crammed into a car and drove three blocks to a cemetery. We eased along the lane, past the small stone maintenance building in the center, and out to a far corner, the black shadow of the wooded mountain that shelved the town. The headlights went off, and we lit up one joint, then another. Led Zeppelin screamed from the boom box lodged in the front seat, and Train kept complaining, jokingly: "Play some real jams, man." He'd take an Earth, Wind, and Fire tape from his pocket, wave it around.

What was his game?

He was fast. One of the "best sprinters in the state," the articles reminded us. And he could jump. He'd swat at least two shots a game, and he was one of the few players in our suburban league who dunked in games. One practice before the season started, the coaches had each player leap and tap a marked board on the gym wall, and then they would scribble down a number. For the record, my vertical leap when I was sixteen years old was twenty-eight inches. Train's was forty.

Race is part of this story, too. Word on the street is that a white dealer turned Train in, got off himself. Such racism doesn't surprise me. I remember my girlfriend and me—an interracial couple—being denied admission to a movie in nearby Danbury. Yet blackness was about not only oppression, but style. Train was one of the two blacks on the team, one of twenty or so in a school of twelve hundred. The whites on the team, myself included, were among the forerunners of the current suburban teenager's desire to be black. Everything Train did was cool: cranking Rick James on his Walkman, wearing leather ties, even sprinkling baby powder on his chest after he showered.

I used to pull hard for Dr. J, and then Magic, over Bird. I remember visiting a girlfriend in Rochester in 1985 during the NBA finals. She was part of an all-black summer program, and we joined the rest of her floor, squeezing into a dorm room. The Lakers won in the closing moments, and we—fifteen blacks and a sympathetic white—went crazy, slapping the walls, hugging one another. Actually, no one hugged me.

I haven't completely escaped my prejudices. Some years ago my brother was explaining why he had been rooting for Arkansas over Duke for the national championship. "You know how it is," he said, "it's hard to like white players." We both laughed, but I knew what he meant.

Perhaps we've seen too many questionable calls, too many obviously racist referees, both on screen and in our own games. After graduating from college I played in New Milford's summer league on a team that had four blacks, most of whom had been imported from neighboring towns. One game we played against a group of clean-cut guys, local athletes, white. At halftime, over twenty fouls had been called on us. They had one.

I am not one to complain to or about referees. That, in fact, was one of only two games I've played in which I felt the referees were deliberately unfair. The injustice made me furious.

We won by one point on a last-second steal and layup, our first lead of the game. I was punching the air with my fist after flinging the pass ahead to a teammate, watching him dribble leisurely ahead of everyone and lay the ball in. I don't usually punch the air.

In high school some weekend nights, a little drunk, a little high, we'd go "carting." We'd cruise into the FINAST parking lot, and one of us would roll down the car window, lean out, and grab a shopping cart. He would pull it alongside the car as we drove off in search of a back road. I don't think I ever held the cart myself.

One night Train was in the car, and he took his turn with the cart. He leaned out the passenger's seat window and entwined his long bony fingers around the metal, black against silver. Andy, the driver, sped up. Those beside me hollered. I did, too, in response to the cart's rattle, the sparks flying from the wheels. Faster and faster, heading toward the bridge. Sixty miles an hour. Train let go and screamed, and the cart hurtled into the darkness.

Looking back, of course it seems insane, especially for Train. Those fingers so valuable, so magical; the challenge so stupid. Still, it was a record—carting at sixty miles per hour; something we would talk about, something we would remember.

I am not a basketball hustler. I couldn't be. I'm not good enough. I could start at point guard for a mediocre high school team right now, although I didn't in high school. In high school, I did not make the team until my senior year, and then I rode the bench—the twelfth man of twelve. Some games, when our team was getting destroyed, my friends in the bleachers would organize a chant—"J.D., J.D.,"—encouraging the coach to put me in. It rarely worked.

This sorry situation originated my sophomore year when my family moved to New Milford, Connecticut, and I started to play basketball after school. Hard to believe now that many of those games I played in long pants—jeans or corduroys or chinos—the same pants that I had worn to school. I'd just fling off my velour top or unbutton my dress shirt and be ready to play. Some of the other players, the real jocks, would have changed into shorts and T-shirts. Others looked like me—longish hair, acne. I must not have seemed like much when I stepped onto the court. In one game, I was guarded by Brian McCarthy, the junior varsity coach (the same man I would coach under at Warren High, years later). I took him to the hole a few times and our team won. "Guess I underestimated him," I heard McCarthy say.

I was one of the few players who shot with one hand, and I remember other players asking how I did it. I didn't have perfect form, but I think I looked more accomplished than those who still relied on their offhand for a little extra push, a habit they had acquired from playing with a big ball before they could fully control it. I had become interested in playing basketball that winter through watching the Knicks on TV, and I shot with one hand in an attempt to imitate Ray Williams and Michael Ray Richardson, the Knicks' guards. In my driveway, I practiced Richardson's peculiar one-handed change-of-direction dribble, a move I don't think I ever used in a game until after I had left college.

Such imitation seems integral to basketball, but it is probably emphasized too much, often at the expense of creativity. And creativity is the game's lifeblood. In a 1984 *Esquire* essay, "The Black and White Truth about Basketball," Jeff Greenfield explains what he labels "black" basketball: "If there is, then, the need to compete in a crowd, to battle for the edge, then the surest strategy is to develop the *unexpected*: to develop a shot that is simply and fundamentally different from the usual methods of putting the ball in the basket." This emphasis on the unexpected can be expanded to every phase of the game: a slight hitch in a crossover dribble, a touch pass. Imitation is valuable and necessary, but finally imitation only is like an artist without ideas, craft without vision.

Almost all coaches, however, want the predictable, the controllable, the repeatable, the fundamentals. And too many players want simply to have the moves of a player that they admire (Be like Mike!). Nowadays, they not only want the same moves as Kobe, but the same sneakers, the same baggy shorts. Patrick Ewing started wearing a T-shirt under his uniform, and suddenly every team seemed to have at least one or two players, usually big men, wearing a T-shirt.

My earliest basketball memory is going with my father to the small University of Massachusetts gymnasium, a building covered with ivy, to watch Julius Erving. I don't remember the game itself, just the warmups. I stared at the basket, counting in amazement the number of balls going through the hoop so quickly. One morning that spring, my father woke me at six. We were going to New York to meet my Uncle Harry and watch UMass play against North Carolina in the National Invitation Tournament (NIT). I don't remember much about this game either. We arrived late and walked through the smoky upper regions of Madison Square Garden for what seemed an hour, trying to find our seats. (Years later, I would use my college ID to buy these same blue seats for half-price—$3.50. I'd drink a jumbo beer and watch the Knicks' Bernard King nail baseline turnarounds.) Midway through the first half, the game was over. Erving had three or four fouls; North Carolina was up by twenty or so. We left early, got some food, went home. I was five.

In Normal, Illinois, where I lived for seven years, until high school, my basketball memories again involve watching more than playing. Illinois State, where my father taught, always had teams vying for a spot in the NIT. Doug Collins played there, but no one player or game stands out as much as the introductions. The lights off, the two spotlights swerving around the stadium, then settling on the free-throw lines, the boos for the opposing players—"Who's he?" the fans would scream in unison.

"Who's he?" Just yesterday I asked that question at the Y to another player sitting on the sidelines. Who was that cocoa-skinned guy— 6'2"—checking Scoonie Penn, Ohio State's standout point guard?

"I don't know." He smiles at me. "He's pretty good."

When you enter a gym, or step through the opening in the chain fence, people look, size you up. They don't look long at me. 5'7". White. I don't have the Cleveland Cavaliers mesh shirt, the baggy shorts. My head isn't shaved. I'm wearing cutoffs and a thrift-store purple T-shirt that reads, in teal lettering,

UWMBDA
University of Wisconsin–Madison
Ballroom Dance Association.

On the back, teal figures of a woman and man dancing, surrounded by teal stars.

I'm no one they know.

⸺

Is there anything as satisfying as when someone recognizes that you can play ball? I make a point of saying "good game" to people who play hard and well, even mentioning a particular skill—"you shot great," "nice job on the boards." I wish I said these things because I truly admired their games, but I do it as much in hopes of eliciting some praise for me. One of my last games before leaving Wisconsin—James Madison Park, Lake Mendota casually lapping the boardwalk just behind the courts—I held out my hand to the best player on the team we had just beaten, a 6'3" black guy who had played in long pants. "Good game."

"Good game," he said back, "*real* good game." Yes.

I think that's why, despite all the miserable games suffered through, all the gunners and bruisers, the threats, the trash talk, the dirty looks after a questionable shot or turnover, a basketball player is always interested in playing pickup against new players. It's hard for me to walk past any basketball game and not join in—even if I've just played for three hours, even if my ankle is swollen and unusable. The thought that these people don't know my game, and that I could introduce it to them, is almost overwhelming.

While I've been injured, I go to the gym and shoot around, see if I still have any moves. Once, I peeked into the gym when a game had just ended. The remaining players were trying to rustle up enough bodies for another game.

"You wanna run?" one asked me. How I wanted to say yes, even though I had been forbidden by family and doctors.

"That man's got game," another said before I could speak, "I seen him shootin'."

"I can't," I answered. Who needs to play, when you can get a reputation just by draining a few practice jumpers? So much of the joy is developing a reputation, generating other players' faith in you, when even those better than you will pass you the ball willingly, trusting you to bring it up and, if they're open, get it back to them. An inbounds pass is a compliment. "You the man," it says. "You bring it up."

———

There is no denying it. The sport breaks you, turns you angry. I want to idealize it, but there are too many games I wish I'd never played, too many players who have made the experience unpleasant. Some journal entries:

A long week. First, at the Bloomington Y, the "Businessman's Basket-ball," 11:30–1:30.

I reject that I was frustrated because I didn't see the ball. I had played two games the week before in which I scored only one basket, shot twice, and I'd enjoyed it. It was the old man (old? fortyish) who was playing. He wasn't horrible, but he had developed a conviction that he could make every call. There are several ways to deal with this. Mine is to be silent—assume, or, rather, allow the game to mean more to him than to me. Still it made me want to stop, and the guy was on my team!

Incident number two: an outdoor court across from the hospital, a court I rarely play on. A tan, Mexican-looking guy, a few inches taller than me. Plays like he lives on the court. Taking and making shots that would only go down there. Decent player. I choose to guard him, and he starts burning me, even blocks a shot of mine. We come back, though. I score a few against his lackluster D, and he heaves up some crazy shots. Most though, we have to give back to him, since he calls fouls on every drive. So it's game point, and he drives the lane. I get help, and he loses control of the ball, catches it a few steps later (maybe he got hit, I don't know). He stands and rolls the ball back to the top of the key, obviously calling a foul, yet not wanting to say it.

"That's got to be a travel," my teammate says, feigning ignorance. He goes to take the ball out.

"Wait, wait, switch that around," my man says.

"You walked, man."

"I wouldn't have walked if I didn't get slapped on my hand." He shakes his wrist, grimacing.

"I didn't touch you."

"Somebody did." That had to be me. I swear to you I had given him plenty of room. I was tired of him calling fouls on me.

"Respect the call," I say, an essential rule for civilized playground ball.

"I made a call, I called traveling." My teammate doesn't want to give in. Of course, the traveling would be nullified by the slap. I'm silent.

The two stare at each other, and my teammate gives them the ball. My man drills a bank shot over me immediately, and they win the game. He says something stupid to my teammate. I pick up my keys and walk off the court.

I don't need it. Egos. I play to have fun, not to watch grown men fight over a ball, a game. I play to compete, too, but not to argue, never to argue. Calling fouls is a last resort, an admission of weakness. You should be fouled so bad that the person who did it calls it for you.

I've taken weeks, even months away from the game, rationalizing them with phantom injuries. Often, I've just become overwhelmed with my obvious failures. The pain of not being good is real. Since moving to Wisconsin, I've suffered through three games in which I didn't score a point. My team lost two of those games. The worst was a half-court game in which my team was up 14-8, game to 15. I, like most players, think that if I really need to score, I can, and as they came closer—10, 11, 12—I increased intensity. At 14-13 I decided to end it. I drove the left side, pulled up and faked, then leapt for a short jumper. The ball trickled across the rim. We ended up losing.

The curse of Bobby Knight has struck. After learning much about the game by coaching under a Knight disciple, and then moving to Indiana, watching IU basketball for six years and playing with Hoosiers in the gyms and on the playgrounds, my one-on-one game has disappeared. I can set picks, hit the open man, and box out, but I can't take it to the hole through two guys, smooth and strong, and I'm hesitant to take any but the most open shots. Here, in Madison, the game is drive and dish. Though there's plenty of nice passing, picks are rare. One must create one's own shots.

Or, perhaps, it's simply the curse of age. I am playing against mostly younger players, and I sense that I'm losing a step. Even if I beat my man on the dribble, I don't usually have the energy to go over or around another and lay the ball in. My main move now is to fake a jumper, then duck under the defensive man and drop a floater in. Sometimes effective, but not a strong move.

<hr/>

Say that Bradley is dribbling hard toward the basket and the defensive man is all over him. Bradley turns, in order to put his body between his opponent and the ball; he continues his dribbling but shifts the ball from one hand to the other; if his man is still crowding in on him, he keeps on turning until he has made one full revolution and is once more headed toward the basket. This is a reverse pivot.
from JOHN McPHEE's *A Sense of Where You Are: A Profile of Bill Bradley at Princeton* (1965)

I've always had reservations about John McPhee's book, which is thought to contain some of the best writing on basketball. McPhee gives a fine character sketch of Bradley, and, with Bradley's help, he details the physical and mental preparations of a superior player. Yet the above description, which is characteristic of the book's prose, lumbers to the hole. It surprises me that McPhee himself played basketball, for his writing lacks the sport's speed and energy. Basketball is a game of colons and dashes, commas and the sweet period of the ball dropping through the net (dunks, of course, may merit exclamation points), but semicolons? Or the clunky, "shifts the ball from one hand to the other." Anything would be better: "changes hands, shifts hands, shifts the ball, switches hands." Some phrasing that captures the move's quickness. Spin move.

Was it just that the language was different in 1965? Or different among different classes? Bradley, like McPhee, is from the white upper class. As McPhee puts it, Bradley overcame "the disadvantage of wealth." Does McPhee's style mirror Bradley's sensibility? Perhaps Bradley's game—methodically honed alone in the gym in Crystal City, Missouri (population 4,000)—inspires this stilted language? Nope. Listen to Bradley himself, quoted by McPhee: "What attracted me was the sound of the swish, the sound of the dribble, the feel of going up in the air. You don't need eight others, like in baseball. You don't need any brothers or sisters. Just you. I wonder what the guys are doing back home. I'd like to be there, but it's as much fun here, because I'm playing. It's getting dark. I have to go back for dinner. I'll shoot a couple more. Feels good. A couple more."

Goodbye semicolons, hello sentence fragments. Look at the repetition in the sentence structure ("You don't need"), the sharp variations in sentence length, the colloquial language. Typing the passage, I got ahead of myself and typed "I'd rather be here." Bradley didn't say "rather"—too stilted. His speech "Feels good."

It may be a while before such speech becomes recognized given the conservative nature of sports literature readers. Charles Stein, reviewing Spike Lee's *Best Seat in the House: A Basketball Memoir*, claims Lee's "account of the game's history is marred by his too-colloquial style of writing. There are too many sentences like this one: 'Never showed any panic, he might have had the ball stolen from him here or there, but not very often, because I can't recall a single case.'" Now Lee's sentence isn't brilliant, but it does seem true to the feel of basketball. Note the dropping of the pronoun, the commas functioning almost like dashes.

Perhaps language helps shape the game itself. English's abruptness seems to capture the stops and starts, the instant change of direction, of the American game. How many more syllables to say the same thing in Italian? Spanish? Take it to the hoop? *Llévalo al grano.* An extra syllable, and all those open vowels. And we wonder why Europeans' drives, their entire games, look slow, drugged.

Yet written English has failed to capture the dynamic of basketball, too, what Greenfield calls basketball's rhythm: "feeling the flow of the game, finding the tempo of the dribble, the step, the shot." Greenfield quotes Bill Spivey, a New York high school star, "It's not a matter of somebody setting you up and you shooting. You *feel* the shot."

Feels good.

Any player will tell you how important feeling into the "flow of the game" is. There are games when you will take the contested eighteen-footer, and other games when you pass up open fifteen-footers. Beyond this general observation, though, it has been hard to articulate this "flow of the game." The written language, perhaps, with its permanence, its drive toward the end of the sentence, doesn't easily bend to the remarkable qualities of basketball, its constant demand for improvisation, its endless combinations. McPhee makes it sound a bit workmanlike, but he captures the essence: "Every time a basketball player takes a step, an entirely new geometry of action is created around him. In ten seconds, with or without the ball, a good player may see perhaps a hundred alternatives and, from them, make half a dozen choices as he goes along. A great player will see even more alternatives and will make more choices." In discussing Bradley, McPhee suggests that "this multiradial way of looking at things can carry over into . . . life." Can it also carry over into language? How to describe the split-second decision-making process that is basketball, to express the myriad possibilities in each second, yet still keep the fluidity and speed that marks the game?

To speak basketball's language may require a shorthand that would be indecipherable to the general reader. This explains my own fragments. I don't want to take this essay to completion. My own writing feels too removed from the game.

Spin moves. It's about creating: creating space, opportunity, beauty. It's about repetition: shooting, shooting, shooting. Crossover dribbles against an imagined defender, the quickest player you know. Take the ball back to the top of the key. Do it again. Pull-up. Let it fly. *Shoot it.* Kick it out. D. D-up. Switch. He's mine. On your left. Let it go. Yo! Shit. Nasty. Sweet. Hit the boards. Box out. Whose man? Whose man is that? Pick up. Pick right. That's it. Nice D. Walk. Call. Ball.

———

I hold the record for highest shooting percentage in the DePauw University basketball intramurals. Four for four, with one three-pointer in ten minutes on the faculty team, playing against some bullyish frat boys. My season ended just before halftime. With the referee counting off the seconds—"seven, six, five"—I dribbled hard upcourt, planted at the three-point line, and collapsed, screaming. One of my teammates said he'd heard a "pop." My no-look pass, meant for a cutter in the lane, glided out of bounds. I swore and felt nauseous, clammy. Eventually, some other faculty players carried me into the training room. The student trainer tested my leg, easing it up and down, then wrapped it in ice and gave me some crutches. Still pleased with my stellar first half, I limped out to watch a few minutes of the game, refused offers of rides home, then drove the half-mile back to my house, the possible seriousness of my injury gradually sinking in.

I had torn my anterior cruciate ligament. I had an eight-month-old son, Aidan, and an alternately sympathetic and furious wife. I was thirty years old.

Two and a half months later, I went under the knife. My brother, Jamie, my longtime basketball cohort (how much hoop have we played/talked together?), had flown out to help Eileen and me through the operation. When he saw me afterward, half-dead from the anesthesia, yellowish white, he couldn't bring himself to lie and say I looked good. Sprawled on the back seat, I threw up in the car returning from the hospital, and Aidan imitated me, coughing.

Those days Jamie visited he read *Foul: The Connie Hawkins Story*, the same book Mark had read feverishly as a boy on the courts of Paterson, New Jersey. Jamie got up at 5:30 to drive me to the hospital after a miserable night in a Motel Six. We had thought it would be easier to stay in Indianapolis, near the hospital, but Aidan couldn't sleep, and so neither could the rest of us. (Jamie, who had no children then, said later that he "learned a lot" that night.) In the waiting room, I put my head back and closed my eyes. Jamie sat next to me and read furiously, the way a starving man eats. When I was wheeled into post-op, groggy and nauseous, the book was still in his hand, a finger lodged in it to keep the page.

I got a phone call from Mark last week. He said he's played once since Christmas, his back has gotten bad. He's forty, and he fears that he may have to hang it up.

Ira Berkow, in *To the Hoop: The Seasons of a Basketball Life*, quotes a friend: "The less time that elapses between the time you are doing something that you enjoy and the time you die, the less time you have been old. Age is a matter of not giving in."

If it were that easy.

When I talk to Mary on the phone, she explains the process: stem-cell harvesting, an experimental treatment for those whose cancer has metastasized. A way to give even heavier doses of chemo. The odds, from limited data: 30 percent live more than a year. Then she asks about my knee. I tell her I feel absurd complaining, then I complain anyway. "It's been over a year. It should be ready to play now. I really miss playing, more than I thought I would."

What a thing to say to her as she anticipates the next stay in the hospital after the chemo weakens her immune system.

"Oh, I know," she says. I hear the energy in her voice. "There's two things I miss: teaching and basketball."

Mary plays basketball well. In our weekly game, she would usually guard men who were stronger and faster than her, but she endured. She boxed out, she made her shots, she set picks. She endured what I would have considered suffering—not being better than my opponent—and she endured it cheerily.

Just the other day, after a year of lifting weights and stair-stepping, I returned to the court, testing out my knee in a pickup game at the Y. I clamped my brace to my leg so tightly that it made me dizzy, and someone who would not have been faster than me two years ago blew past me, even drilled a jumper in my face. I almost walked off the court, disgusted with my failures: bad passes, a missed layup.

My team lost two out of three. I felt sick. I lay on my back, unable to focus on the ceiling, on anything.

Things change. We endure.

I vow not to get depressed when I've been beaten. We all get beaten. The cartilage in my knee will grind and crack, and I will set my picks, box out. Every once in a while, I'll still make a slick move, a no-look pass, and I will imagine the fleeting thought in the minds of my opponents and teammates: *This guy's pretty good.*

Once, Mary blocked my shot at Bryan Park. No mean feat in our group. Fred, the 6'5" buzz-cut redhead, a good athlete, blocked my shot once and screamed, "Yes! I've been waiting three years for that." I'm quick enough, coordinated enough, and cautious enough to hardly ever get blocked, but one time, on a short jumper in the paint, Mary got all ball, tied me up. For the record, Mary T. Lane stuffed me. Something to remember.

A year after we had moved from Bloomington, Eileen and I, toting our three-month-old son, Aidan, returned for a day, a Saturday. Mark and I would go play at Bryan Park, and then Mark, Colleen, Mary, and Dave would go out to lunch with Eileen, Aidan, and me. We parked outside our old house and went in to see Mary. She was finishing her chemo, and it looked like her cancer was going into remission; everything seemed better. We set down Aidan, asleep in his car seat, and exchanged hugs.

In a few minutes, Mark appeared in the screen door, just as he had when I had lived in the house, and soon he and I were walking down Fess Street's cracked, uneven sidewalk. Occasionally, Mark gave his ball a hard bounce. It was very hot, but I wanted to play—to remind everyone, and myself, how good I was, to remind them, and myself, how it used to be.

And, I had a mission.

For a few days in late summer in 1995 at Bryan Park, you could have gone down to the basketball courts, looked up over the backboards on the eastern side and seen a pair of bright red high-top sneakers in the sky. They dangled from the telephone lines that sliced through the park. (Sneakers over telephone lines are a tradition in Bloomington. Twenty or thirty pairs are always hanging from the wires that cross Grant Street near the White Mountain Ice Creamery.) This pair was mine. Ripped at the ankles, with small holes worn through the bottom, they were no longer wearable. My signature. Bright red. When the games were finished that Saturday, and everyone was staggering to the bathroom for water, or dragging themselves to their steamy cars, I tied my laces together and flung the sneakers up over the wires—first shot.

A few moments later, I realized that my keys were in them. I borrowed a ball, knocked them down, removed the keys, and then, after a couple tries, relanded them. Then I walked up the hill, crossing the jogging path for the last time, and headed toward the house that was no longer my home.